THESE
STONES
REMAIN

THESE STONES REMAIN

60 REFLECTIONS ON FINDING HOPE WHEN DARKNESS LINGERS

CLAUDIA CAMPBELL

These Stones Remain

Library of Congress Cataloging-in-Publication Data

LCCN: 2024906167 (paperback) ISBN: 978-1-961732-23-0 (ebook) | ISBN: 978-1-961732-21-6 (paperback) | ISBN: 978-1-961732-22-3 (hardcover)

Published in association with Called Creatives Publishing, www.calledcreativespublishing.com

Cover design: Called Creatives Publishing

Interior design: Claudia Campbell

2024 – First Edition

For Noah, Caleb & Micah:

The precious minutes of your entire lives have forever changed the way I live mine. One day closer sons.

For Eliana & Nia:

You are continual reminders that God still does miracles.

You bring me uncontainable joy.

For Andrew:

Thank you for being my constant.

Thank you for not only gathering the stones alongside me but also shining a light on those that remain in darkness.

Thank you for never giving up on me. You are my greatest gift on this side of eternity.

TABLE OF CONTENTS

FOREWORD

Life can be challenging, no doubt.

Our family has faced and overcome numerous challenges over the years, yet we know we live in a broken world and there is more that lies ahead. Throughout it all, my wife, Claudia has stood as an ambassador of hope. This hope is not rooted in the ordinary but in a deep faith in a God who knows us intimately, is before all things, and holds all things together.

I recall a time when Claudia was enduring excruciating pain from her current illness, and I sat beside her, feeling helpless and lost as a husband. Despite countless prayers, and even after a recent surgery, the pain persisted. I was heartbroken and I cried out to God asking how long? I questioned why this suffering lingered, and wondered if we were being punished for something that we had done wrong.

As I prayed, I reflected on the man who was born blind in John chapter 9. When Jesus encountered this man, his disciples also thought that surely, he or his parents must have committed a sin that led to this suffering. But Jesus replied, "Neither this man nor his parents sinned, but it was so that the works of God might be displayed and illustrated in him" (John 9:3, AMP).

Witnessing Claudia's agony, I had lost all hope. But even in pain, Claudia made a request I'll never forget: to keep worshipping God amidst her anguish. Doubtful and discouraged, I hesitated but her unwavering encouragement to me personally, revealed her God-given ability to uplift others in their darkest moments.

In these pivotal times, Claudia felt compelled to document and share how God pointed her to hope when life was just too much to bear. It became so clear to me that God would be glorified in and through our story.

In "These Stones Remain," you will find a devotional and prayer journal that shares some personal stories as Claudia invites you to gather the memorial stones that are scattered in life's toughest moments. These stones will serve as reminders of God's enduring presence and goodness in suffering.

In these pages, you are encouraged to embrace gratitude and the hope that is possible as you navigate through seasons of adversity.

This hope is Jesus! And I pray that you are forever changed as you encounter the one who enters into your brokenness, and holds you close as he heals your heart.

~ *Andrew Campbell*

INTRODUCTION

I should be dead. Really, I should. But God!

As I sit in the stillness of another sleepless night, I remember that there is no medical reason that I should still be alive. I have had so many close calls with death, and there have been many nights, just like this one, where I lie awake in excruciating pain.

I have battled severe Endometriosis, a chronic and often invisible disease since I was a teenager. And like so many others, I can't remember a life without pain. I got so used to the pain that, at some point, I stopped believing in God for the healing and abundant life he promised in John 10:10 and became content with simply surviving.

I had plans to write this book on the other side of pain. Instead, I am writing in the midst of it. I wrote many words sitting in my recliner on a heating pad, eating a tub of ice cream. I wrote others on Saturday mornings when I sat in bed with the shame of my condition piled on top of the physical pain. My children watched cartoons and ate bananas for breakfast while I poured out words and prayed they would help someone else feel seen. And as I wrote in anguish, I compiled an ever-increasing list of questions for God, wondering if he'd ever answer. He just seemed silent.

But I realize it is okay not to have answers in the waiting. When I gave up my desire to fix everything, I stopped fighting the darkness and rested in the light of Jesus, which always found its way to me.

My story includes a continuous battle with waiting in the dark, and it coincides with the life story of my high school sweetheart and husband, Andrew. Together, we have journeyed through depression, chronic illness, infertility, grief, and special needs parenting. We experienced our first loss due to a miscarriage. Our lives were plunged into deeper mourning one year later when we lost our three sons, Noah, Caleb, and Micah, whom we held in our hands for a brief time before they went to spend eternity dancing with Jesus. After years of heartache, we are raising two daughters, Eliana and Nia, who are constant reminders of God's faithfulness. Our girls were both diagnosed with Autism Spectrum Disorder at an early age, and through their lives, we continue to encounter more of Jesus and his goodness each day.

We have spent the last few years trying to embrace the beauty of living and loving while shielding our hearts from the ongoing pain of inconsolable grief.

We learned that joy shows up when we open our eyes to the everyday goodness of God right where we stand. Joy isn't something we look forward to on the other side of pain, and it is not an award for winning after wrestling with grief. Joy is present in the presence of Jesus and is available to us at all times, even while suffering, because Jesus himself is our joy.

"So Joshua called together the twelve men he had chosen—one from each of the tribes of Israel. He told them, "Go into the middle of the Jordan, in front of the Ark of the Lord your God. Each of you must pick up one stone and carry it out on your shoulder—twelve stones in all, one for each of the twelve tribes of Israel. We will use these stones to build a memorial. In the future, your children will ask you, 'What do these stones mean?' Then you can tell them, 'They remind us that the Jordan River stopped flowing when the Ark of the Lord's Covenant went across.' These stones will stand as a memorial among the people of Israel forever."

JOSHUA 4:4–7, NLT

Early in my struggles, God had me jot down reminders of his truth I found in the hardest of times. These became my stepping stones, my twelve memorial stones. They became reminders of times when the Lord stopped the rivers of endometriosis, infertility, depression, and even death that physically overwhelmed me. They reminded me of his faithfulness, strength, mighty power, and love that carried me across on dry land in his everlasting arms.

My obstacles became my stepping stones.

As I cried out to God for answers, I realized that while he did not always respond in the way I wanted, I could always see him. He was the ultimate miracle I desperately wanted, and his presence was always the answer to my prayer. For this, I truly did pray.

While reflecting on the last few years, I realize it's easy to proclaim the goodness of God after walking through a season of despair and basking in the joy of answered prayers. But what about praising while we are in the midst of our pain? Will we look around to see the evidence of his goodness when faced with difficult circumstances? Will we identify the stones of remembrance he has placed in our lives as reminders of his faithfulness while the storm rages, threatening to erode our foundation of truth?

This book holds the hope I have held on to over the years as I surrender to his sovereignty when life is too much to bear. You'll read my testimony as I endured a season of affliction that spanned over two decades. It is the story about a God who, even in the hardest times, would leave me stepping stones that would become a path to remember his goodness. This book is a guide to help you pray and reflect as you seek joy in a life that includes waiting, pain, and struggle.

> "There is no such thing as darkness with you. The night, to you, is as bright as the day; there's no difference between the two."

PSALM 139:12, TPT

Because darkness and light are alike to God, he is with us during our brightest moments and our midnight mourning. During your season of waiting, you may only see the darkness of your current circumstances, but he sees the light. Not only does he know the light to come, but he sees the light in the middle of darkness. I pray this book encourages you to keep striving to find the light of our Savior, even if the night seems long.

> "He made darkness his secret place..."

PSALM 18:11, NKJV

God's secret place is in the darkness. If this is where you find yourself, I encourage you to look around right where you are—because that's where you will find him. It was in the darkness of my circumstances of sickness, pain, depression, and barrenness that God gave me a new view of his faithfulness.

As you journey through this book, you can trade your burdens for the beauty of the hope you'll find when you open your eyes, hands, and heart to the extravagant joy that has the name Jesus!

How to read this book:

In each section, I share a story of when God visited me and deposited a stepping stone of remembrance that kept me going. I share five of my favorite verses associated with each memorial stone as I invite you to reflect on your stones and encourage you to pursue "THIS" in the middle of your story.

What's THIS?

In each section, as you pray, I want to encourage you to find THIS:

T – Thanksgiving: A posture of gratitude as we declare he is good and recall his goodness to us personally. This prayerful thanksgiving practice builds trust in his continued faithfulness in our lives. It will give us hope.

H – Hope: We will declare that God is indeed our hope as we pray through his promises for our lives. We will seek his face for tangible signs of hope in the challenging times. We will declare abundance in our current circumstances because we know he is here with us.

I – In the midst of: We will cry out to our Heavenly Father as we ask him to show up and meet us in the midst of the heavy parts of life. We know God is often evident to us in the good times, but we will ask him to open our eyes as he reveals himself to be a loving Father who comes alongside us in our suffering.

S – Surrender: We will declare our surrender to his sovereignty. Our "nevertheless" moment as we say, "Not my will but yours be done" (Luke 22:42). We will rest in our obedience to the Father and look to him. We will rely on his grace to sustain us instead of depending on the fruit.

As I write this introduction, I am sitting in the waiting room at the doctor's office with yet another health scare, and I am not sure how this story will unfold. There are so many unknowns. When I called my earthly father to lament, he said, "Wait to worry, and in your waiting, reflect on his past faithfulness." So, as I wait, I am giving thanks as I recall his consistent faithfulness in my life.

This **thanksgiving** is giving me divine strength for today and leading me to a bright **hope** that even **in the midst of** this current unknown, I can **surrender** to his will because I know "all things work together for good." (Romans 8:28, ESV)

In Joshua 3, as Joshua led the people of Israel into Canaan, they came upon the Jordan River, which stood between them and the Promised Land. God instructed the priests to step into the flowing river. As they took their steps of faith, he would cause the rivers to stop flowing, but they had to walk in and wait for the miracle. This book is for the one walking and waiting for the miracle, hoping that the water would stop flowing. I'm inviting you to step in and trust that God will fill your heart with joy as he leads you on dry land to "THIS."

The enemy doesn't want you to cross over the challenges you are currently facing. He prefers that you sit on the sidelines and live a life of surviving instead of thriving. This book is an invitation for you to put down the stones of fear and doubt that are weighing you down and instead pick up these memorial stones as you declare that you will see the goodness of the Lord in the land of the living (Psalm 27:13).

You likely have this book in your hands because you or someone you love is going through a hardship. Before you turn the page, I want you to know I am sorry. This book will not have the answers to all your questions, that is not the intent. But I am writing to let you know you are not alone. I pray that the following pages point you to the one who has seen, heard, and can identify with your pain. He is the one with all the answers. I encourage you to trust once more in the God who is who he says he is and does what he says he will do.

God's plans for you are so much bigger than your dreams. I pray that the twelve stones in the pages ahead will boost your faith and propel you into a life of abundance and joy as you pursue THIS!

ONE:

STONE

OF

provision

STONE OF PROVISION

As a young child, I worried a lot. Frankly, I still do. One of my dad's favorite phrases in moments of my anxiety was, "Don't worry. God will provide." He is a man filled with faith, and while I'm sure there are times he's struggled with the how and the when, he has always been certain of the outcome. As I have matured, I have realized that statement to be true. I cannot remember a time when God abandoned us.

> "Once I was young, and now I am old. Yet I have never seen the godly abandoned or their children begging for bread."

PSALM 37:25, NLT

I know Jesus to be Jehovah Jireh, the Lord who will provide, yet there have also been seasons of drought. Oftentimes, these moments will lead to doubt, anxiety, and worry. While I know that he will ultimately come through for me, just as he has promised, sometimes, in the face of struggle, it's hard to recall that God has met our every need.

If you are in a season of waiting on manna from Heaven, I want to remind you that God sees you, hears you, and knows your heart's desires.

As you rest in and reflect on this stone of provision, I want to invite you to think about what you are asking the Lord to provide for you at this moment. Is it financial? Is it a community to laugh, lament, and do life with you? Do you need him to provide a path out of a difficult situation?

I want to pray with you concerning his provision in your life.

T: Father, I thank you that you have never forsaken us. Thank you for being faithful in providing for us daily in every area of our lives. As I remember your faithfulness, help me to trust in you instead of worrying about my tomorrow.

H: Father, I know you do not withhold good things from those who trust in you. Help me to hope in you despite my current circumstances.

I: Lord Jesus, it feels like I've been waiting on this for a long time, and sometimes, it's hard for me to keep asking. Help me to know it's okay for me to keep coming to you and that you desire to sit with me in the midst of my hoping and waiting.

S: Help me to rest in your sovereignty and to surrender my desires into your capable hands. Help me remember that you will always work it out for my good and your glory.

For this, I prayed.

yet i have
never seen
the righteous
forsaken

psalm 37:25

FRIENDSHIP

Two people are better off than one,
for they can help each other succeed.

ECCLESIASTES 4: 9–10, NLT

Have you ever met someone for the first time and immediately embraced them, knowing that you won't only be friends but will be family forever?

Twenty years ago, I moved from my home in Jamaica to start my career as an actuary in the United States. I was young, I was scared, and I was all alone. I was blessed to grow up in a very close-knit family and had never been away from them. Honestly, I wasn't sure how long I would last. As I boarded the plane, my parents said to me with tears in their eyes, "You can always come back home."

Before I arrived in the United States, another Jamaican actuary at my new company heard I was coming. We did not know each other, but in the hotel lobby on my first night away from home, I met Michelle and her future husband, Stafford Jr. We embraced instantly, and they have been my chosen family since that day.

During the early years of my career, not only did I struggle with being away from home, but there were times I wondered if I was good enough to succeed in my job. There were many moments when I wanted to admit defeat and go back home, but my new big brother and sister would not let me quit. I remember when my brother Stafford bought me a fleece jacket before my first winter. At the time, I had no idea how much I would need it. But it became a symbol of not just something that would keep me physically warm but a reminder that when the world gets cold, the Lord will send friends who will stand with you, lift you, and not let you fall.

The beautiful thing about true friendship is finding people who know you at your lowest and still love you anyway.

I am grateful God has provided friends to walk with me during each step of the journey to remind me that *he is not just a Father but also our best friend.* He is a friend who loves and cares for us even when we stumble in sin. He sends people to strengthen and encourage us in the hardest of times.

As you meditate on his provision of friendship, I invite you to consider this:

T: Reflect on a time when God gave you a great friend. As you write, give him thanks for his provision.

H: As you reflect on God's past faithfulness, ask him to open your eyes and show you a tangible sign of hope. Ask him to remind you that he is not just your Father but also your friend.

I: What are some of your desires concerning friendship? Sit at God's feet and seek his face in the midst of your current needs. He wants to know what is on your heart.

S: Are you currently in a season of loneliness? What would it look like to surrender this to God? How does it make you feel knowing he will never leave you alone?

For this, I prayed.

HOW MUCH DO YOU HAVE

The disciples replied, "Where would we get enough
food here in the wilderness for such a huge crowd?"
Jesus asked, "How much bread do you have?"

MATTHEW 15:33-34, NLT

What do you do if God asks you to give up the very thing for
which you've been waiting?

"Send her your peonies." It was a clear instruction.

In our home, we are always in a waiting pattern for peonies. After
we lost our sons, my husband planted peonies in their honor, and
it took years before they bloomed. As I struggled with chronic
pain, our daughters would say I was waiting on the peonies. They
noticed that whenever they bloomed, I would always muster up the
strength to leave the bed to see them and behold the beauty that
reminded me of our sons.

Our peonies are done by July each year, but there is one particular
place that always has peonies in the fall. Each year, I wait with
anticipation for notification of their fall peonies. As soon as the
email came this particular year, I went to order them. But as I was
about to checkout, God said, "Send her your peonies."

I had a friend going through a tough time, and the Lord told me I
should send them to her. At the time, I knew I didn't have enough
money to buy two orders. I was torn because I had been waiting on
these peonies for months. But the instruction from God was clear.

After I purchased them, she found out several family members were terribly ill, and the flowers arrived on the same day as things became challenging in her home.

God knew in advance that she needed the peonies.

Shortly after, I got a note from my favorite flower shop thanking me for my support over the years and giving me a credit that I could use to buy peonies for our home as well. Even though they were later than I hoped, they arrived in the middle of a difficult week. God knew in advance that I needed them, too. He made a way for me to purchase twice the number of peonies.

Dear friend, how much bread do you have?

Is it possible that in yielding to the Spirit at work within us in obedience, his mighty power can multiply the plans we hand over to him and produce a divine overflow of provision?

I invite you today to rest in the one who knows what we need in advance. Because God provides, what you have in your hands may be much less than what you think you need, but we serve a God who multiplies.

As you meditate on his provision of multiplication, I invite you to consider this:

T: Reflect on a time when God has surpassed your expectations. As you write, give him thanks for multiplying his provisions.

H: As you reflect on God's past faithfulness, ask him to open your eyes and show you a tangible sign of hope. What would hope look like for you at this moment?

I: Where are you currently experiencing lack in your life? Seek God's face in the midst of your current needs. He wants to know the desires of your heart.

S: What would it look like to surrender your needs to God? How does it make you feel knowing he will always provide, even if it looks different than you imagined?

For this, I prayed.

A WAY OF ESCAPE

No temptation has overtaken you that is not common to man. God is faithful, and he will not let you be tempted beyond your ability, but with the temptation, he will also provide the way of escape that you may be able to endure it.

1 CORINTHIANS 10:13, ESV

A few years ago, I received a job offer for a director position with a new company. It was not my ideal job at the time, but I considered it because, frankly, it offered more money. As I prepared to accept the offer, the company pulled it at the last second. I remember my husband saying, "You went ahead of God on that one. It was not what you needed." Yet, I was quite disappointed and felt I could have made it work. I couldn't understand then that God had provided me with a path of escape in advance.

Six months later, the same company reached out to me unsolicited to offer me a senior director position in a different department. This new position was much more significant and one I did not feel qualified for. But God!

As I grew and developed in the position, there was a total restructuring in the company that led to job reductions. While my position was fortunately not affected, the director role that I almost accepted was eliminated.

We serve a God who sees ahead of us and provides a way of escape in advance.

Our Father desires us to rely on his spirit to guide us in a life of abundance. However, there are times when waiting on his provision is hard, and we jump ahead into less-than-ideal situations because we are human. But I want to remind you that the enemy's snares will not overtake you because God is faithful even when you are tempted!

If you currently find yourself wanting to give in to temptation, you are not alone. Speak to your Father. Ask him to help you wait on him and to provide you with his peace as you rest in the knowledge that he knows your tomorrow and will always provide for you.

As you meditate on him providing a path of escape from temptation, I invite you to consider this:

T: Reflect on a time when God has been faithful to provide you a way of escape.

H: As you reflect, ask him to open your eyes and show you a tangible sign of hope. What would a way of escape look like for you at this moment?

I: Where do you need his guidance while waiting for his provision? Ask God to help you and give you wisdom as you wait on him.

S: What would it look like to surrender your plans to God? How does it make you feel knowing that even in the most difficult circumstances, he will help you endure?

For this, I prayed.

YOUR EVERY NEED

And my God will supply every need of yours according
to his riches in glory in Christ Jesus.

PHILIPPIANS 4:19, ESV

The promise that my God will supply every need is one that I have held on to in every season of my life. It is a reminder that he is not just the God of Abraham, Isaac, and Jacob, but he is my God. He doesn't just consider some of my needs, but he desires to fill all my needs.

When we lost our sons in 2013, those were our last embryos from previous cycles of In Vitro Fertilization (IVF). We had maxed out every credit card available to us and could not afford another cycle. Mentally and emotionally, I did not have the strength to try again. On the other hand, Andrew wanted us to try one more time. He kept insisting that he heard the Lord say, "One more time," but we had no more money.

As we resigned ourselves to the fact that we could not afford another IVF cycle, we didn't realize the truth that the Lord was preparing to fill this very need. Then, one day, we received a check in the mail that we were not expecting. I had no idea my employer from seven years prior owed me money. They had an audit and a cleanup effort, and as a result, we received a check that was enough to cover our last cycle of IVF.

It was that cycle that led to the miraculous birth of our daughters.

I think of Abraham as he prepared to sacrifice Isaac in Genesis 22. He had no idea that a ram was already approaching as his provision. When my husband heard from the Lord, he had already prepared the check and had it on the way. The Lord had already provided before he gave my husband the word. Knowing that we did not have the finances, it would take great courage for him to ask me to try again after the heartbreak of losing our three sons. But he heard from the Lord. When the check came in the mail, he looked at me and, with tears in his eyes, said, "One more time."

The Lord knows your needs before you ask and has already provided them.

I want to join you in trusting that your Heavenly Father has heard your every cry, seen your tears, and will overwhelm you with his provisions because he is your Shepherd, and you shall lack nothing in him. (Psalm 23:1)

As you meditate on his provisions for your every need, I invite you to consider this:

T: Reflect on all the times God has provided for your needs. As you write, give him thanks for his provision.

H: As you reflect on his past faithfulness, ask God to open your eyes and show you a tangible sign of hope. What would hope look like for you at this moment?

I: What do you need from God today? Ask him. He wants to know the desires of your heart.

S: Open your heart and hands as you surrender to God today. Ask him to fill you with more of him as you wait on his provision.

For this, I prayed.

COMMUNITY

Even so, you have done well to share with me in my
present difficulty.

PHILIPPIANS 4:14, NLT

When we were pregnant with our daughters after years of
infertility, at 20 weeks, my water broke. After our previous loss, the
doctors thought it was nearly impossible for me to have a full-term
pregnancy. Even then, our friends stood with us and believed —
even when the odds seemed stacked against us.

Sometimes, we don't recognize or acknowledge the people walking
alongside us during a challenging season. And that for these
people, this is their fight as well. They laugh, cry, pray, and praise
God with us. They indeed share in our difficulties, and they never
give up.

One of these friends is my dear friend Zara. There was a time when
it seemed that my and Andrew's faith was at a breaking point as we
struggled to believe. Zara showed up determined to paint the girls'
nursery. She had already decided these girls were coming, that they
would live and not die and would need a cozy room to call their
own. Zara even painted the stripes I always wanted. While she
will tell you that she never wants to see stripes again (if you've ever
painted stripes, you might agree), Zara would also say she would do
it all over again because she believed!

And that, my friend, is the power of community. On the days when
your heart is doubting, you can lean into the faith of others. A
friend's faith can increase your faith and help you keep going.

While every Christian's journey is personal, Jesus never intended for us to be alone.

When you are going through challenges, the enemy wants to keep you isolated, but that is not the desire of your Father. He loves you so much that he will send people to come alongside you and love you deeply.

Dear friend, I pray that the Lord will send you a community that will sit with you and share with you in your present difficulty. I pray that in your current season of waiting, he will reveal himself to you through a community that gives you strength for today and bright hope for tomorrow.

As you meditate on his provision of community, I invite you to consider this:

T: Reflect on a time when God has been faithful to send you a friend who believed. Give him thanks for a community.

H: As you reflect, ask him to send you a tangible sign of hope in the form of someone to encourage you in your current season.

I: Ask God to help you with your unbelief. Ask him to remind you of his past faithfulness and to encourage you with his presence.

S: What would it look like to surrender your doubts to God? Ask him to strengthen you in your moments of weakness.

For this, I prayed.

TWO:

STONE
OF
protection

STONE OF PROTECTION

We recently went on a vacation to a water park, and on the last day, my daughter decided she wanted to conquer her fear of the big water slide. Andrew loves water slides and immediately suggested that we all do it together, but the thing is, I am terrified of water slides. Even though he promised he would be there to protect us, I refused. But my daughter insisted on going with her dad. When I reminded her that the inside of the water slides would be dark, she responded, "But Dad has promised to hold on to me, and he always keeps his promises." That's when it hit me: *Her protection was in the promise.*

Twice, she successfully went down the slide with her dad! And while it was dark, he held her in his arms the entire time.

"He will cover you with his feather. He will shelter you with his wings. His faithful promises are your armor and protection."

PSALM 91:4, NLT

When you trust in God's ability always to protect you, you are not just holding on to the promise, but you are holding on to the one who has never broken his promises. Even when you doubt you will make it through, your protection is in the promise. And the promise is only certain based on the one who is making the promise.

Eliana knew I was afraid, so it would have been useless if I had made her the promise. However, her dad was confident, so she believed in his ability to keep her safe despite her fear.

My friend, do not allow the uncertainty of your darkness to supersede the promise of protection he made to you in the light.

Our God is not only bigger *than* the darkness but also bigger *in* the darkness.

Can I pray with you concerning his protection?

T: Father, I thank you for your promise of protection. Thank you for being faithful to cover and shelter us in every season. As I reflect on your promises, help me trust in you as my fierce warrior and protector, and never forget that you are bigger than my fears.

H: Father, your word says in Job 11:18 that having hope in you will give me courage. It reminds me that I will be protected as I rest in your safety. Help me never to forget that my hope is in you.

I: Lord Jesus, I can't see. It feels so dark, and I can't find my way. I desperately need your protection. Help me know that even in the darkness, you are my safe place, and as you hide me under your wings, you are covering me on every side.

S: Help me surrender my circumstances to you. Abba Father, none of this is a surprise for you. Help me rest in your sovereignty and trust your heart and love for me even when I cannot see.

For this, I prayed.

His faithful
promises are
your armor &
protection.

psalm 91:4

HOW LONG

How long, O Lord? Will you forget me forever? How long will you hide your face from me?

PSALM 13:1, ESV

"How long, Lord, how long?" was the cry of my heart after two decades of chronic pain. I have suffered from chronic pain since I was a teenager. It wasn't until we were unsuccessful in trying to have children that I was finally diagnosed with severe, debilitating endometriosis.

For so long, I was bedridden and struggled to do basic tasks to facilitate daily living. My husband, Andrew, did everything around the house while also being my primary caretaker. Once we were blessed with our daughters, he also cared for them. We struggled for so long to become parents, but once we did, I could not be the mother I desired to be because I was in so much pain. I was exhausted, miserable, and jealous of others who could do all the things I struggled to do. I wanted relief, and my continuous cry was, "How long, Lord, how long?"

After many years and multiple failed surgeries, I finally found an expert specialist out of state. The surgery revealed my body contained severe infections that should have given me sepsis. But God! There was no reason for me to be alive. Still, somehow, the same adhesions from the endometriosis that had taken over so many of my major organs had formed a barrier around the infection that prevented it from spreading throughout my body.

The very disease that caused me so much pain was keeping me alive.

In my season of despair, as I cried out to God, he gave me divine protection in my waiting. God had not forgotten about me and protected me, even in my sorrows.

Psalm 13:6 continues with praise: "I will sing to the Lord, because he has dealt bountifully with me." These scriptures remind me that I am not alone in my cries of desperation. I am not alone in wondering, "How long?" and neither are you.

Even on your worst days, the Lord is with you, and he is for you.

With each long night of pain, there was a morning after. And each new day came with the reminder that I somehow survived the darkness of the night. Even as I cried, the Lord made it possible for me to survive each day because he was beside me, protecting me every step of the way.

Dear friend, you may feel abandoned, rejected, or forgotten. You may be exhausted, but you are not alone. Your Father has seen you in your weakness. You don't have to be strong today. Exhale and relax into the arms of the one who is your shield and your refuge, the only One whose arms are tender enough to embrace yet mighty to defend and protect you from any plans of the enemy. Rest in him.

If you are currently in a season of lament, feel free to cry out to God even as you consider this:

T: It's hard to find thanksgiving while lamenting. I want to invite you to reflect on the reminder in Scripture that your heart can still trust in your good God even amid your tears. When you are ready, thank him for still protecting and guiding you even when you feel that he is far away.

H: As you reflect, declare that God is your hope in your "how long?" season. Ask him to show you tangible evidence of his beauty and to give you joy as you rest in the safety of his mighty yet tender arms. What would hope look like for you at this moment?

I: Where do you need God's protection today in the midst of your cries? Run into the arms of Your Father and tell him where you feel forgotten.

S: What would it look like to surrender your cries to God? How are you comforted with the knowledge that there is divine protection even in your waiting? When you are ready, write some words as a song unto the Lord as you rejoice in his salvation and sovereignty.

For this, I prayed.

DIVINE INTERRUPTIONS

I know what I'm doing. I have it all planned out—plans
to take care of you, not abandon you, plans to give
you the future you hope for.

JEREMIAH 29:11, MSG

I recently had a work trip canceled with less than 24 hours' notice
before I was supposed to depart. I was annoyed. After weeks of
planning, and making preparations that would make the event
a success, suddenly, without warning, I watched my hard work
become wasted time.

A few days later, when I should have been returning home from
the meeting, an unexpected snowstorm grounded all flights out of
that location. If I had traveled, I would not have been home in time
for my daughter's dance recital.

I was grateful for God's protection and for his divine cancellation.
None of this was a surprise to God. There is such comfort to be
found in the words, "I know what I'm doing. I have it all planned
out."

Pause for a moment, take a deep breath, and inhale, saying, "My
Father knows what he is doing." Then, exhale: "He has it all
planned out." I pray that his promise to always care for you gives
you hope in today's impossible situation.

Friends, there is no promise this life is going to be easy. We receive
no assurance of when it will all work out. But we are promised that
it will work out for our good. (Romans 8:28). I am so grateful he

didn't answer my prayers to go on that work trip. I am so thankful his plans superseded my preparations.

"...No eye has seen, no ear has heard, and no mind has imagined what God has prepared for those who love him."

1 CORINTHIANS 2:9, NLT

This experience reminds us that even when we don't understand, God has a plan in advance of our prayers. These plans are to protect and take care of us and sometimes shield us from life's unexpected storms.

God has a purpose. God has a plan. He knows what he is doing.

As you meditate on the stepping stone of protection through his divine interruptions of your plans, I invite you to consider this:

T: Reflect on a time when God has gone ahead and intervened in your plans. As you write, give him thanks for his divine protection.

H: As you reflect, ask God to give you peace as you hope in him while processing the news of your current interrupted plans.

I: Where are you currently battling with unmet expectations? Express your frustrations to your Heavenly Father even as you ask him to sit with you in disappointment.

S: What would it look like to surrender your preparations to him today? Ask him to help you always seek him and his wisdom as you align your plans to his will for your life. What are you holding on to that could be protection from the Father hidden in your pain?

For this, I prayed.

IN DEEP WATERS

Do not be afraid, for I have ransomed you. I have
called you by name; you are mine. When you go
through deep waters, I will be with you. When you go
through rivers of difficulty, you will not drown.

ISAIAH 43:1-2, NLT

When my grandfather passed away, I was devastated. All my life, I was blessed to have all of my grandparents, and when he died, it felt like a gut punch to the stomach. Later that year, my other grandfather passed away.

A few months later, my father-in-law and my cousin's infant child passed away the same day, hours apart. Then, several months after those tragedies, we heard the words "endometriosis" and "infertility," indicating it would be near impossible to become biological parents. The years that followed were rife with excruciating pain, multiple surgeries, miscarriages, and failed cycles of IVF.

It truly felt like deep waters, rivers, and fires of oppression. It was one thing after another, then another. We thought we were getting pummeled, yet still, God was our shield, and he was our protector.

Your Heavenly Father knows the struggles you are currently facing, and he is reminding you not to fear. You are his beloved. He has called you by name. He will protect you. He will not let you go.

There are no promises that Christians will have an easy life, but we do have the assurance we will never be alone. One of the reasons we share our stories is as a reminder of the times God has shown up for us before. This passage reminds us of the time he parted the Red Sea (Exodus 14), comforting us with the truth that he has protected us before and he will do it again.

As I write this, I must confess I am so exhausted. I feel like I have been overwhelmed with so many darts on every side. I am exhausted. Financially, physically, and emotionally, I don't feel I have much left. The only thing keeping me going is reflecting on the times when it seemed like the waves would consume me, but God showed himself to be my shield and protector. He has revealed himself to be mighty.

"Mightier than the thunders of many waters, mightier than the waves of the seas, the Lord on high is mighty!"

PSALM 93:4, ESV

Dear friend, do not be afraid. The Lord, your God is mighty!

As you meditate on his protection as you are overwhelmed with attacks on every side, I invite you to consider this:

T: Reflect on a time when God has been your shield and delivered you from the enemy's snare. As you write, thank him for how he has kept and protected you.

H: As you reflect, put your hope in the hands of your mighty Father! Ask him to help you replace your fear with hope. Hope in him and in his ability to shield and protect you from fiery attacks.

I: What battles are you currently facing? Name them one by one, and as you do, ask God to give you victory over each one. Ask your Daddy to give you peace as you rest in the knowledge that he will be your shield of protection.

S: What would giving your battles to God look like today? Ask him to remind you of his promises concerning every situation you face. As you rest in his sovereignty, write these verses and his promises as a sign of surrendering your fears to his faithfulness.

For this, I prayed.

PRIZED POSSESSION

There once was a shepherd with a hundred lambs, but one of his lambs wandered away and was lost. So the shepherd left the ninety-nine lambs out in the open field and searched in the wilderness for that one lost lamb. He didn't stop until he finally found it. With exuberant joy, he raised it up, placed it on his shoulders, and carried it back with cheerful delight!

LUKE 15:4-5, TPT

When I was at my lowest during my battles with infertility and endometriosis, I spiraled into a pit. Depression engulfed my mind like an oppressive enemy. Many nights, I turned off my phone, got in my car, and drove. I secretly wished to be washed away by the storms that consumed my mind. I couldn't see a way out.

After driving for hours, alone and hurting, I'd turn my phone back on to find hundreds of missed calls from my dad and husband. Even when they couldn't get me to come home, they would not stop pursuing me.

Their constant pursuit is a reminder of the Father's heart for me. God chased me and protected my heart with his love whenever I ran away. Broken and hurting so deeply, I could only be held, protected, and mended by the one who knew me intimately and created my heart.

In the parable in Luke 15, Jesus talks about a shepherd's pursuit of his treasured sheep. In the same way, *you are his most prized possession.*

You are more precious than rubies, and God will search high and low to get to you. He will not stop pursuing you, my friend. God's love for you will protect you. And with exuberant joy, he will lift you on his shoulders and bring you home with cheerful delight!

If you are in a place where you are feeling far away from God today, I invite you to allow yourself to be found by him. He is not pursuing you to scold or shame you but to rescue, save, and shower you with his delight, joy, and love. Rest, my friend, and let him find you today.

As you meditate on the stepping stone of protection found in his love, I invite you to consider this:

T: Reflect on a time when you felt lost. How did God show up in your life? Did he send a friend or family member your way to remind you of his love? As you write, thank him for how he has protected and pursued you with his love.

H: As you reflect, put your hope in God's banner of love. Ask him to help you find joy in his delight for you.

I: Where do you find yourself running away from God amid your suffering? Ask him to help you pause, stop running, and then allow him to find you.

S: What would it look like to surrender, stop, and rest in God in the middle of your wilderness today?

For this, I prayed.

NOW AND FOREVER

The Lord will protect you from all harm; he will protect
your life. The Lord will protect your coming and going
both now and forever.

PSALM 121:7-8, CSB

My daughter Nia is a runner. Her challenges with autism make
it difficult for her to sit still. Over the years, we've had very close
calls with her because she starts running when triggered by lights,
sounds, or anything distracting.

Once, she left the building at school without the teachers realizing
she was gone. Another time, she ran away from my husband in a
parking lot and almost ran in front of a car. Once on vacation, Nia
slipped away from the adults, and we couldn't find her for several
minutes. Without a doubt, the protective hand of the Lord has
been on her life since she was born. Indeed, he has protected her
from all harm.

Recently, I decided to take both girls on a walk around the
neighborhood alone. I hesitated because I wasn't sure if I could
keep up with her if she got triggered and decided to run. But I had
to trust that the same God who has protected her thus far would
continue to be with her and with us on our walk.

**Your God has gone before you, friend. He will protect
your coming and your going. He is beside you not just
now but also in your future.**

In this world of uncertainty and close calls that may be around the corner, the Lord has promised to be close to you in the good, bad, and ordinary. He is here in your present and is already there in your forever. And while this does not ensure your life will be free of problems, it confirms that you will never be far from his protection.

As you meditate on his protection from all harm, I invite you to consider this:

T: Give thanks to the giver, the keeper, and the protector of your life for shielding you in the past, in your right now, and in your forever. Reflect on a time when God delivered you from harm.

H: As you reflect on your Father Emmanuel, who will protect you from all harm, what does it look like to put your future hope in him? Ask him to show you a sign of his goodness in your present moment that you can hold on to in the forever portion of your journey.

I: Where are you on your journey today? Where do you need God's protection in the unknowns of tomorrow? Your Father is present and protecting you every step of the way. Let him know what you need. He wants to hear from you.

S: What would it look like to surrender your life to him today? Can you let go and trust the close calls of your life into his sovereign hands? Let him know that no matter what comes your way today, you will trust that he holds you and your world in his hands.

For this, I prayed.

THREE:

STONE
OF
peace

STONE OF PEACE

"Even if things do not go the way you have planned, I am still God. I am still good. I am still sovereign. Can you trust that? Is that good enough for you? Or maybe the real question is, am I good enough for you? In your perceived failures in the eyes of man, will my delight in you be enough for you to keep going? Will my presence in your pain be enough to bring you peace? My child, I am here. In the midst of your pain, I desire to be your peace."

Those were the audible words of the Lord that came to me during my darkest hour.

After we lost our sons, I wondered how I would continue with life. We were basking in the miracle that we were pregnant with three boys, and we looked forward to the day we would see them be born and grow up in the knowledge of the one who loved them even before they were conceived. Then, in a matter of hours, they were gone.

How could God possibly get glory out of this story?

Over the following weeks and months, I realized that he never left me, even when I pushed God away. God was good not just after the manifestation of the promise I had so desperately wanted, but he was and still is good in the middle of the darkness. There was no way I could have survived losing them without having his peace.

Peace is not reflective of a life that is free of suffering.

Peace and pain can coexist. I can say this because I have lived it and know it to be true.

I'm in pain. My sons should not be dead. And yet, God is with me still. He is still good.

At the time, this was all I knew to be true. And today, as I still grieve the loss of my sons, I also know these statements to all be true.

In the middle of my sadness, I had many questions and didn't get many desired answers. The reality I face is not the way I would have written the story of my sons' lives, one which included their deaths so quickly after their births. Yet, because of the resurrection, it became a story of earthly births and deaths instantly traded for eternal life with him. And because they are with him, and because he sits with me, he became the answer to my questions. As the tears flowed, his tangible presence kept me going.

I became intimate with the God who was greater than the miracle we were seeking. He became my peace, and this peace overpowered my pain. It is this power that ultimately strengthens me every day. God is your peace, and even now, he desires to sit with you.

As you meditate on the stepping stone of his peace, I want to offer you this prayer:

T: Lord, I thank you for being my peace in a life of brokenness and pain. Thank you for coming alongside me and being a constant in my life. Even though I still have so many questions, thank you for always showing up and being my answer.

H: Help me never to lose hope. Remind me that your resurrection is not just the foundation of my peace but also my strength for today and my hope for a brighter tomorrow.

I: I am in the middle of a fight for my sanity and my life. Jesus, please be my guide. And when the storms are just too much to bear, please remind me that you will always be my peace.

S: Help me surrender my questions to your sovereignty. Help me never to forget that even in this, you will get the glory. Because you know the end from the beginning and the tomb is empty, death and pain will never have the final say.

"Now may God, the fountain of hope, fill you to overflowing with uncontainable joy and perfect peace as you trust in him. And may the power of the Holy Spirit continually surround your life with his super-abundance until you radiate with hope!"

ROMANS 15:13, TPT

For this, I prayed.

now may god,
the fountain of hope
fill you to overflowing
with uncontainable joy
and perfect peace

romans 15:13

DO NOT BE TROUBLED

I am leaving you with a gift – peace of mind and heart.
And the peace I give is a gift the world cannot give.
So don't be troubled or afraid.

JOHN 14:27, NLT

My husband got very sick a few months before I started writing this book, and there was one night in particular when I had to call an ambulance. As he left for the emergency room, I saw my daughters visibly shaken, and one of them was in tears. As I looked over to comfort them, my daughter Nia held her sister's face between her hands and said:

"Ellie, are you concerned? It is okay to be concerned. I am concerned too. But you do not have to be worried or afraid. Because Jesus died and he rose again, everything is okay."

As soon as she said this, she went to bed and slept peacefully. I was astonished at what she said. But she was correct!

You see, because she has autism, my daughter Nia only sees things in black and white. With her, there is no gray area. So, in her mind, the truth that she has learned about Jesus from the Bible should give us peace of mind and heart. Period.

For her, that truth was greater than the facts of her current situation. There was no gray area—it was either black or white. My daughter reminded me that his resurrection will always be enough!

Oftentimes, we think of peace as a result of our current circumstances. But that is not the gift of peace that Jesus refers to in this passage. He speaks of a peace that surpasses human understanding (Philippians 4:7). This peace rests on us, abides within us, and we find it in him.

The ESV translation of John 14:27 says, "My peace I give to you." This peace is a reminder that we are not alone in our challenges. When Jesus came and dwelt among us as a human, he suffered, was mocked, and abused. He sees and understands and has walked through the troubles of this world, yet he had peace and gives the same peace to us today.

Give your concerns to him, dear friend, and let him give you the gift of his peace.

As you meditate on the stepping stone of his peace in times of trouble, I invite you to consider this:

T: Give God thanks for being your peace. Thank him for the gift of his son, who walked among us and is not a stranger to the trouble you face today.

H: As you reflect on God's gift of peace, how does that give you hope? I pray your expectancy is increasing even now as you remember his resurrection is forever a sign of eternal hope.

I: Take a moment to express your current need. Where are you currently troubled? Ask God to help your unbelief despite your worries and fears.

S: Surrender your fears at the feet of Jesus. Rest in his spirit, and let his peace surround you on every side.

For this, I prayed.

TAKE HEART

*I have told you all this so that you may have peace in me.
Here on earth you will have many trials and sorrows. But
take heart, because I have overcome the world.*

JOHN 16:33, NLT

As so many of us battled the challenges of the worldwide pandemic in 2020, there was undoubtedly an overflow of trials and sorrows. It felt as if we were all holding our breaths, just waiting to exhale after being isolated for so long, but we didn't know how for some reason. I kept waiting for the other shoe to drop because it seemed like that had become the norm.

Christians have no promise of a life free of trouble. In fact, we can count on just the opposite. We will have many trials. I've often felt that we do The Gospel a disservice by not talking about our challenges of today and those that are sure to come. And while we cannot always find a way out of our sorrows, the beauty of the gospel is we find our trials sandwiched between the two truths in this verse.

You can have peace in Jesus.

Because he has overcome the world.

Since Jesus has assured us of his peace and overcoming power, while we may not be able to break out of our prison walls, the Prince of Peace can come in. And that is where we find our hope and courage. This certainty in our Savior is how we take heart.

Sometimes, the testimony isn't that you broke out but that the one whose name is Peace broke in.

It's the story of a God who pursues us and promises us his peace before the trials even come. And with his peace, we can take heart because we know he wins.

As you meditate on the stepping stone of his peace and the one that has already overcome the world, I invite you to consider this:

T: Give God thanks for the promise of his peace even before the trials come your way.

H: As you reflect on God's peace, can you rest and find hope in the truth that he has already overcome the world?

I: Take a moment to think of everything causing you to worry. Ask God to show you the peace found in him for each of your trials.

S: Can you trust in God's sovereignty in your current sorrows? How can the truth of his peace and victory that sandwiches your trial lead you to surrender as you take heart today?

For this, I prayed.

IN ALL THINGS

Now, may the Lord himself, the Lord of peace pour into you his peace in every circumstance and in every possible way. The Lord's tangible presence be with you all.

2 THESSALONIANS 3:16, TPT

We were on our first vacation to Anna Maria Island in Florida some time ago. While we were there, I decided I would not miss a sunset. The sunsets there are stunning. One day, it rained for hours, but shortly before it got dark, the rain broke up, and we rushed to see if we could catch the sunset. As we left to head down to the beach, the girls saw their first-ever rainbow, which was a double rainbow! That rainbow, in duplicate, was a tangible reminder of God's promise.

A few short hours later, we got the phone call that my mom was rushed to the hospital. She was frighteningly ill. She was bleeding uncontrollably, and it didn't look like she would make it. We were terrified. It happened out of nowhere.

As the tears started falling, God reminded me of the sign he showed me right before we got the news. His tangible presence was evident in that double rainbow. It was as if he had poured out his peace before our circumstances.

By the grace of God, after several weeks of battling for her life, my mom made it back home to us. When I asked her how she felt in those near-death moments, she said, "I had no fear. It was as if the Lord had poured his peace on me."

The peace written in 2 Thessalonians 3:16 is a constant state of peace. And I wondered, what would it look like for us to remain in this posture? This perfect peace is only possible if we fix our eyes on the Perfecter of our Faith and seek daily to live a life filled with his Spirit.

I am so grateful that God, in his kindness, sent me a tangible reminder of his promise before that storm. That rainbow filled me with peace even when I would soon be scared.

My prayer for you, dear friend, is that God will send you a tangible sign of his love, which will be just what you need in your current circumstance. I pray you feel the peace of the Father being poured all over your life.

As you meditate on the stepping stone of his constant peace at all times and in all things, I invite you to consider this:

T: As you reflect, thank God for his constant peace – supernatural peace that he pours out on us at all times and in all things.

H: Ask God to show you a tangible sign of his presence to fill you with hope as you rest in him and his peace.

I: It may be hard for you to feel God's peace in every area. Take a moment to share your doubts with him. Ask him to reveal himself during your current season of waiting or despair.

S: Surrender your eyes and your heart to God. Ask him to help you do this daily, filling you with his Spirit and constant peace.

For this, I prayed.

EXILE

And work for the peace and prosperity of the city where I sent you into exile. Pray to the Lord for it, for its welfare will determine your welfare.

JEREMIAH 29:7, NLT

I've worked for a few companies throughout my career, but there was one in particular where I struggled. I struggled with the work, with the culture, and with the people. I was miserable. In many ways, it felt like I was in exile. I wanted to close my eyes and hold on long enough for the season to pass. But it wasn't passing.

I remember conversing with my dad, who said, "Build there. Work the ground."

"Seriously?" I thought. I certainly did not want to build there. I struggled just to settle. So now what?

A few weeks later, I was in a meeting where it was clear that a colleague needed encouragement. At first, I kept quiet, but then I felt the Lord whispering, "Build right here." I spent some time on the phone listening and encouraging, and as I did, I felt a weight lift. As I was offering peace to my colleagues, the Lord was also gifting me with his peace.

Many of us are currently walking through periods of exile—at our jobs, homes, and schools. Sometimes, it is hard to consider these spaces as breeding grounds for increase. But I believe the Lord will open our eyes and give us opportunities to see we all have something in us we can offer to add beauty and value to where we are right now.

If you are looking for peace in your current circumstance, I invite you to plant seeds of joy, settle here, work the ground, and build here. Seek his extraordinary peace in your exile.

As you meditate on the stepping stone of his peace in your time of exile, I invite you to consider this:

T: As you reflect, thank God for his promise in Jeremiah 29:11, that of a future and the hope waiting for you on the other side of the exile. Thank him for the strength to build and settle in a difficult time.

H: Ask God to fill you with his hope, especially when your trust dwindles.

I: Express to God how hard you find it to settle here. Give him your thoughts and ask him to send you people to encourage you throughout your exile.

S: Surrender the current situation to God. Trust that even in this, he has a plan for your peace and prosperity.

For this, I prayed.

BE MY GUIDE

For you shall go out in joy and be led forth in peace...

ISAIAH 55:12, ESV

One night, I went out on a date with Andrew, and on our way home, suddenly, rain started pouring. It was raining so hard we couldn't see anything. As we drove, my husband said, "In every season, you have to keep your eyes open and be on guard. Do not forget the signs God sends you as markers to guide you in the light. You will need them to lead you on the days when the tears have flooded your eyes and it's too hard for you to see."

I have spent many years walking through different periods of darkness. I have found that in times when I am unable to see, it is helpful to remember how God has previously led me into the light. If I am always walking with and being led by him, my guide in the darkness becomes bigger than the darkness itself. And that guide is his peace.

We are led in peace when we know that nothing in our future will catch God off guard.

He is in complete control, and we can trust him not just with our today but also with the unknowns of our tomorrows. When we allow him always to be our guide, his peace leads us through all life's troubles.

"You keep him in perfect peace whose mind is stayed on you because he trusts in you."

ISAIAH 26:3, ESV

As you meditate on the stepping stone of his peace, I invite you to consider this:

T: As you reflect, thank God for the times he has guided you in the light and shown you the way out of a tough situation.

H: Ask God to remind you of this hopeful path as he continues to guide you on the days when you are unable to see.

I: Tell God your struggles with doubt and fear. Ask him to help you fix your mind and gaze on him in the middle of your unknowns.

S: Each day, seek to surrender your path to God. He is faithful to lead and guide you as you place your trust in him.

For this, I prayed.

FOUR:

STONE
OF
faithfulness

STONE OF FAITHFULNESS

The week I started writing this book, I lost most of the vision in my left eye. Out of nowhere, I was suddenly struggling to see. I was scared. And I couldn't help but notice the irony. My vision was becoming impaired, rocking my faith right as I sat down to share with you how God has shown me his faithfulness in the darkest times.

"For we walk by faith, not by sight."

2 CORINTHIANS 5:7, ESV

While this scripture has never felt more real, it was not what I wanted to experience at the time. How was I supposed to declare God's goodness as I was literally sitting in the dark? In those moments, I knew I had to trust in his character as I held on to the promises that he gave me in the light. The only way to walk by faith is to believe in his faithfulness.

Just as the flowers that bloom come from buried seeds or the birthing of eternal life in a tomb of death, so much of the good that exists today comes from that which we cannot see.

Our dreams often occur with our eyes closed because our vision tends to make us lose focus on reality.

The reality is that we all believe in a future we cannot see. Good or bad, life or death, hurt or hope, peace or pain—we do not know what lies ahead, so we trust the faithfulness of the one who knows our tomorrows. We hope in the one who has transformed darkness by conquering the grave. We rest in the unfailing love of a God who holds all things together.

Dear friend, God is faithful because that is his character.

> "God is not man, that he should lie, or a son of man, that he should change his mind. Has he said, and will he not do it? Or has he spoken, and will he not fulfill it?"

NUMBERS 23:19, ESV

Even if things are falling apart in your world, I want to encourage you with this: God will not lie. He will not fail. Our entire Christian walk is built on the never-ending love of the one we do not see yet believe. Trust that his love for you will continue to work all things out for your good, even when you cannot see.

As you meditate on the stepping stone of his faithfulness, I invite you to consider this:

T: Reflect on a time when God has been faithful to you and your family. How have you seen evidence of his love for you, even in a tough time?

H: As you reflect on God's faithfulness, I want to encourage you to walk outside if possible. Can you see him bringing beauty out of the darkness in your surroundings? I invite you to take a deep breath as you pray, "Lord, give me a sign of your hope."

I: Where are you currently struggling to see God in your life? Bring your requests to him. He sees you. He hears you. He loves you.

S: What would it look like to surrender your visions and plans to God? I want to encourage you to lift your hands to him as you declare, "Lord, help me to trust in your faithfulness and believe in your character when I cannot see."

For this, I prayed.

for the lord is good
and His love endures
forever; His faithfulness
continues through
all generations.

psalm 100:5

AND WE KNOW

And we know that for those who love God, all things
work together for good, for those who are called
according to his purpose.

ROMANS 8:28, ESV

"And we know…" These words from Paul have been at the forefront
of my mind for many years. I often recite them to comfort me
when I am in the middle of a crossroads, challenging my faith.
This verse tells us that at all times, even in suffering, even when it
doesn't seem good, we know that all things are working together
with a purpose that will ultimately be for good. But I must admit,
when facing life's unknowns, I don't always act as if I know this.

I previously mentioned that when my mother fell ill while we were
on vacation, it was sudden and without warning. She had severe
blood loss and deteriorated rapidly. However, during that time,
there was a blood shortage in our home country of Jamaica. Our
family called on social media for blood donations and prayers.

The response was overwhelming, and over a few days, we stopped
counting after we received 40 units of blood. Ultimately, the
amount of blood donated in my mom's name saved many lives that
weekend. And by the grace of God, after a difficult hospital stay
and recovery, my mother survived!

We cannot always understand why we must endure such
challenging times. And even as we live in a fallen world filled with
brokenness and heartache, we know that bad things happen to
good people.

We serve a faithful God who uses those bad things and turns them around for good.

As you meditate on the stepping stone of his faithfulness in all things, I invite you to consider this:

T: Reflect on a time when God has been faithful through a bad situation. How could he use it for the good of others and his glory? Give him thanks for his faithfulness.

H: As you reflect, ask God to restore your hope.

I: In the middle of your brokenness, ask God to show you his strength.

S: Pray that God will give you rest as you surrender. Ask him to help you trust that he is working in this for your good. Ask him to remind you of what you know.

For this, I prayed.

HOLD ON TO HOPE

Let us hold fast the confession of our hope without wavering, for he who promised is faithful.

HEBREWS 10:23, ESV

We struggled with infertility for six years before we first got pregnant. As the months and years passed, we started to lose hope. I would pray for strength each day and for God to send us a tangible sign to encourage us in the days ahead.

Before we were pregnant with our sons, I remember when I had lost all hope and was ready to give up. But then a friend shared with us a dream she had. She told us of the two little girls who would be our daughters, and she specifically remembered them having thick, curly hair. I held on to that word and bought two little dresses as I trusted that one day, I would see the manifestation of that promise in our lives.

When we found out we were expecting triplet boys, I packed the dresses away because, surely, I would not need them. But after our sons passed away, I found those dresses and clung tightly to them, soaking them with my tears as I pleaded for God to fill them.

I realized over time that before he filled my arms with baby girls, he filled those dresses with hope and peace as he was healing my heart.

Many years later, shortly after our daughters were born, they wore them to church for the first time, "for he who promised is faithful."

While I did not know at the time how our story would unfold, the encouragement from my friend that led to those two little dresses restored my hope in the faithfulness of God. They were a reminder that God is with me.

God is mighty. He does the impossible and keeps his promises.

I don't know what you need today, but if you need hope, I want to offer up some of mine. The confession of our hope is Jesus, the one who died and rose again and whose promises concerning the will and purposes for our lives cannot fail. Do not give up.

Even now, God is holding you in his mighty hands. You can trust him. He won't let you down.

As you meditate on the stepping stone of his faithfulness, I invite you to consider this:

T: Reflect on a time when God has been faithful to encourage you through a friend when you needed it.

H: Ask God to show you a sign of hope that will strengthen you today.

I: Are you in the middle of an impossible situation? I am standing with you as you cry out to our faithful God.

S: What would it look like to surrender your situation to God today? I pray that God would heal your heart and fill you with more of him even as you rest in his sovereignty.

For this, I prayed.

NEW MERCIES

But this I call to mind, and therefore I have hope:
The steadfast love of the Lord never ceases; his
mercies never come to an end; they are new
every morning; great is your faithfulness.

LAMENTATIONS 3:21-23, ESV

At the start of second grade, my daughter had an assignment at school to complete the statement, starting with, "I am…" She wrote, "I am never giving up."

I cried when I saw it. I've mentioned previously that my daughter Nia has autism, and throughout her young life, many people have given up on her. I cried because, as her mom, I often wonder who will love her through the tough days. I cried because I often fear that people will give up on her learning ability if she starts screaming or doesn't sit still. I cried because as she got older and stronger, I knew I couldn't lift her and rescue her from a difficult situation. My tears were not for my pain today but my worries for her tomorrow.

Nia has never stopped fighting to learn and function in a society where many see her as different. After an awful day, she can wake up the next morning and start fresh as if nothing had happened the night before. She refuses to give up on herself. And God has never given up on her either.

Nia received a student of the month award at the end of second grade. And once again, I cried.

I cried because it reminded me that God loves Nia more than I do, and his love for her never ceases. I cried because she got that award after several tough months prior, and it was such a reminder of his mercies that are new each day. I cried because it was a reminder that even when my physical arms can no longer lift her, the Lord will continue to carry her as he has been doing all along.

God is faithful to grant you a fresh dose of his love and mercies each day.

On difficult days, I encourage you to view your present struggles through the lens of your past victories. I pray that this will bring you hope.

Today may be challenging, but tomorrow is coming. And while we may not know what the future holds, you can trust God's faithfulness will meet you there.

As you meditate on the stepping stone of his faithfulness that is new every morning, I invite you to consider this:

T: Take a moment to pause and recall your past victories. Give God thanks for the last time you had a good day.

H: As you reflect, pray God will use this memory to strengthen you and bring hope to your heart today.

I: View your struggles today with this renewed hope. Ask God to meet you and remind you of his love, mercies, and faithfulness toward you.

S: What would it look like to surrender your tomorrow to God? Can you rest in not knowing the future but seeking to rest in the will of the one who does?

For this, I prayed.

KEEP WATERING

Unless a kernel of wheat is planted in the soil and
dies, it remains alone. But its death will produce many
kernels – a plentiful harvest of new lives.

JOHN 12:24, NLT

Andrew does an exceptional job at keeping our yard beautiful. We
had a tree taken down in our front yard, leaving a huge hole, so he
decided to fill it and try planting some grass in its place. For two
days he worked, transferring two thousand pounds of dirt into that
hole. Once finished, Andrew planted some fresh grass seeds and
started watering them diligently, hoping to have a beautiful lawn in
the coming months. But after a few weeks, there was no sign of life.

Andrew eventually realized that the seeds he planted were not the
best for the soil he used. Unfortunately, there was no way he could
remove all that dirt and start over. I begged him to abandon the
project because he was wasting his time watering a hole filled with
two thousand pounds of soil, day after day, but he refused to stop
trying.

"If even one seed sprouts, it could multiply," he said. "There is still a
chance."

My husband worked in the yard for another three months before
seeing grass sprout. Then, a few months later, he saw the lawn he
envisioned. Over those months of not seeing any progress, Andrew
decided to be faithful in the watering instead of focusing on the
fruit.

Sometimes, we desire to see fruit, but we are unwilling to sacrifice our timelines, plans, and dreams when things do not go according to plan. We plant the seeds, but we are not willing to let our ideas die so we can see God's harvest in our lives.

Do we believe in his faithfulness enough to be faithful to the call even when we don't see the fruit? Is the faithfulness of God sufficient to trade our definition of success for obedience and surrender?

Dear friend, I pray you will surrender your will to God today. I pray that you can focus on being faithful over fruitful as you rest in his faithfulness.

As you meditate on the stepping stone of his faithfulness and how it can lead you to be faithful, I invite you to consider this:

T: Give thanks to God for being faithful even when you are not. Ask him to help you keep his faithfulness at the forefront of your mind as you endeavor to obey his will for your life.

H: Reflect on the hope of the harvest that is in Jesus. Where can you see his harvest in your life today?

I: Place your seeds before the Lord, even before you prepare to surrender your will to him.

S: Ask God to help you be faithful and diligent in watering the seeds even if you are not seeing the fruit. Pray that he would help you surrender your idea of success to his sovereignty.

For this, I prayed.

COME HOME

And while he was still a long way off, his father saw
him coming. Filled with love and compassion, he ran to
his son, embraced him, and kissed him.

LUKE 15:20, NLT

"You can always come home."

That is what my father said to me with tears in his eyes as I
prepared to leave home in Jamaica to work in the United States of
America at twenty years old.

Being the only sibling living far away from home has been
challenging. I haven't been there to help in the family business
and wasn't around to help when my parents got sick. When my
grandparents passed away, I could only come home for a few days
for their funerals. After we had our daughters, traveling home
became even more challenging. Now, I try to go home once a year.
And still, all these years later, when I go home, my parents throw
special celebrations and treat me as if I never left. They welcome
me with open arms and treat me like royalty.

In Luke 15, Jesus tells the parable of a son and a father who reunite
after the son has been away from home. In this story, the son left
home and fell into a world of sin as he wasted all his money. Even
so, his father not only welcomed him back with compassion, but he
also ran towards him with open arms.

And while some of us are blessed with the love of earthly parents,
nothing compares to our heavenly Father's love and compassion for
us. The arms of your Father will forever embrace you even when the

world turns its back on you and even after you have turned your back on him.

Dear friend, God is faithful. Nothing will ever diminish his love for us, even when we screw up and are not faithful. And no matter where you find yourself in this moment, God runs towards you, ready to embrace you. Fall into the arms of your Father today.

As you meditate on the stepping stone of his faithfulness even when we are not faithful, I invite you to consider this:

T: Imagine yourself falling into the arms of your heavenly Father. As you rest in him, thank him for his unfailing love and faithfulness.

H: What would putting your hope in God's faithful love look like today? How does it help you not to feel alone and know you can return to him, even if you find yourself straying?

I: If you are straying into sin today, I want to encourage you to run to your Father. Tell him where you are struggling, fall on your knees in repentance, and ask him to help you overcome temptation.

S: Sometimes, it is hard to run toward God after you have turned your back on him. You may want to hide, but I hope you will accept the Father's love and faithfulness today instead of hiding. He loves you and is waiting for you to come home to him. Ask him to help you never be afraid of his embrace.

For this, I prayed.

FIVE:

STONE
OF
promises

STONE OF PROMISES

"Let us hold tightly without wavering to the hope we affirm, for God can be trusted to keep his promise."

HEBREWS 10:23, NLT

When our daughters were diagnosed with autism, we were devastated. Honestly, we feared what this would mean for our girls' futures. It challenged our faith. We had already been through so much trying to become parents, and I thought things would get easier. We did not have family nearby and didn't feel equipped to parent children with special needs alone. It felt like God had broken his promises.

Jesus tells us in John 16:33, "In this world you will have trouble." Reading that passage reminded me trouble, trials, and sorrows are not a possibility but a certainty. But that same verse ends with Jesus extending hope when he says, "But take heart! I have overcome the world."

God's promise isn't a life free of trouble but that our trouble is not bigger than the one who has already overcome this world.

How do we take heart?

For me, taking heart looks like recalling all the promises God has already fulfilled in my life and remembering the promises God has given us in his word.

"But then I recall all you have done, O Lord; I remember your wonderful deeds of long ago."

PSALM 77:11, NLT

As I stared into the eyes of my miraculously birthed daughters, considering my diagnoses of endometriosis, infertility, and a toxic womb, and who brought joy to a marriage that had experienced more bad times than good times yet was still standing in the face of grief and pain, I fell to my knees in gratitude. When we are facing a new challenge, it is essential to take time to remember God's goodness and his grace.

I hold on to the truth that "No matter how many promises God has made, they are "yes" in Christ. And so through him the "amen" is spoken to us to the glory of God." (2 Corinthians 1:20)

As I sat with his goodness and his truth, I reflected on these promises:

- God answers prayers. (Mark 11:24)
- God is always with us. (Matthew 28:20)
- God has a plan. Nothing is a surprise to him. (Jeremiah 29:11)
- God works all things for good. (Romans 8:28)
- God will cause us to overflow with joy. (John 15:11)
- God will restore, support, strengthen and establish. (1 Peter 5:10)
- God gives strength to the weary. (Isaiah 40:31)
- God holds all things together. (Colossians 1:16)

Dear friend, I wish I could tell you I had the answer to a life free of suffering and pain, but I don't. Instead, I offer the hope of Jesus and his promise to hold and love you in and through it all.

God is good—he does great wonders, and his love endures forever (Psalm 136). And for all the bad news that you might get along the way, this is always good news. In fact, it's better than good news. It is great news. I pray you hold tightly to his hope-filled promises and find yourself awe-filled at him and his great power at the end of your trial.

As you meditate on the stepping stone of God's promises, I invite you to consider this:

T: Lord, we are grateful that you give us promises for every circumstance and keep your promises.

H: Help us hold tight to this hope without wavering. Help us always put our trust in you.

I: Even as we stand amid trials and sorrow today, give us strength and help us rest in you.

S: Help us surrender to you today. We know that even in this, you will cause all things to work for our good and your glory. Make our joy overflow regardless of our circumstances.

For this, I prayed.

for He who
promised
is faithful
hebrews 10:23

IN ITS TIME

Yet God has made everything beautiful for its own time.

ECCLESIASTES 3:11, NLT

Every year, we plant dozens of bulbs in our garden in anticipation of a bed of beautiful tulips to welcome spring. As I sat on the porch one day, I noticed that, as the flowers started to emerge, they sprouted at various times.

These were individual bulbs, all the same flower, all planted at the same time, in the same garden, and exposed to the same water and sunlight. Yet, the flowers were all at various stages of growth. While each unique tulip bloomed on its timeline, the outcome was the same for all—every tulip bloomed beautifully.

If I had abandoned the promise of the flowers that had not yet manifested, or if I had cut some tulips prematurely because I was focusing on the success of others, I would have missed the opportunity to find joy in the expectation and anticipation of what was to come.

God is good, and he is good to me. But sometimes, as a human living in a broken world, it is hard to hold on to the promise without a tangible sign of things to come. There are times I find myself praying as David did in Psalm 86:17, asking God to show me a sign of his goodness. And because God is so kind, he allows us to taste and see his goodness in the promises he fulfills for others. Often, this makes it easier for me to trust in his promises toward me.

God has already made all things, not some things, beautiful. In him, nothing is incomplete. Everything is appointed not in our timing but in its own time and predestined by the one who knows the end from the beginning.

Wait on his promises, my friend.

As you meditate on the stepping stone of God's promises always fulfilled at the right time, I invite you to consider this:

T: Give God thanks for his promise of making all things beautiful. As you praise him, you are giving gratitude to the Promise-keeper, even if you cannot yet see what you are praying for.

H: Where can you thank God for his goodness in the lives of the people around you? Ask him to show you a sign of goodness that will encourage you while waiting for him.

I: Even as you wait, ask God to remove any thoughts of comparison but help you appreciate the beauty instead.

S: Surrender your timing and your plans into God's hands. Ask him to help you trust in his will for your life.

For this, I prayed.

HIS EYES, HIS HEART

I will instruct you and teach you in the way you should go; I will counsel you with my eye upon you.

PSALM 32:8, ESV

When Andrew decided to teach our daughter how to ride a bicycle without training wheels, she was scared. He promised he wouldn't let her fall. When Andrew noticed she was getting the hang of it, he removed his hand from the bike's control. Though she was doing fine, our daughter got mad at her father.

"You didn't feel my hand, but where were my eyes?" he asked her. "Wasn't I the one that stopped you from falling?"

Eliana had to learn that sometimes, the courage to step out comes down to trusting that her father would not leave her side. She had to be confident that no matter what, he would always run alongside her and would not let her fall.

As I watched them, I thought about the promises of God. I began to desire a deeper level of confidence in my heavenly Father. I remembered how God loves us and promises to come alongside us.

I remember that even when I can't feel his hand, I can trust his eyes and know his heart.

"Wasn't I the one that stopped you from falling?" God reminded me.

Dear friend, I want to encourage you to allow God to lead you and show you which paths you should take and which decisions you should make. You can trust he will not leave you alone in this world. God sees you— his eyes are on you. (Psalm 32:8)

As you meditate on the stepping stone of God's promise to always have his eyes on you, I invite you to consider this:

T: Give God thanks for always leading and never leading you astray. Thank him for being a loving Father that comes alongside you.

H: What would it look like to hope in the gaze of the Father today? Can you rest in his heart when you can't feel his hands?

I: Even as you walk along the paths that God has instructed, pray that the posture of your heart will enable you always to hear his voice.

S: Pray that you would surrender your desire for complete control today and that your heart would remain soft to accept his leading, correction, and love.

For this, I prayed.

NO MORE AFFLICTIONS

...Affliction will not rise up a second time.

NAHUM 1:9, NKJV

When pregnant with our daughters, we vacationed for Mother's Day weekend in Nantucket. We were having a wonderful time. The night before we were scheduled to leave, without warning, my water broke.

We were devastated. I was only 22 weeks pregnant, about the same time as my previous pregnancy, when I went into premature labor, and our sons passed away. What made things worse was that we were on an island with no ferries out until the following morning.

We were about to lose our girls, too.

While I cried all night my husband prayed just one prayer. "Lord, I believe in your promise that affliction will not rise up a second time."

Very little fluid was left when we made it to the hospital the following morning. Because we were not yet 24 weeks along and I was not in active labor, they sent me home to wait for what would naturally happen.

But the supernatural happened.

The sac resealed, and my fluid levels miraculously increased. Months later, my daughter Nia was delivered fully sealed in her sac.

As I write this, I am awaiting a new chronic illness diagnosis – a blow I did not see coming. After walking through endometriosis and living a relatively pain-free life for the last few years, I'm scared of what will come. I admit I have shed many tears. But my husband? He is still praying the same prayer.

Dear friend, I do not know how this story will end as so many unknowns remain. I don't know if I will be miraculously healed from this one, but I believe that the afflictions of mental anguish, fear, and despair will not arise this time. I believe in God's promise of supernatural peace even in this as I give him thanks for the tangible reminders that nothing is impossible with him.

As you face uncertainty today, for a second or third time, I want to encourage you to proclaim peace as you rest in his promises. God will not allow you to be overwhelmed!

As you meditate on the stepping stone of God's promise not to overwhelm you with recurring afflictions, I invite you to consider this:

T: Thank God for his promise not to allow the rivers to overwhelm you. Thank him for his peace during the storms.

H: It may be hard to hope today. If it would help, please borrow some of my hope. You are not alone.

I: As you face yet another challenge, sometimes it is hard to believe. Cry out to God and ask him to help your unbelief.

S: One of the hardest prayers for me is what I refer to as my "nevertheless" prayer. If you would like, I invite you to pray with me. "...Father, if you are willing, remove this cup from me. Nevertheless, not my will, but yours, be done." (Luke 22:42, ESV)

For this, I prayed.

BUT AFTERWARD

"What I am doing you do not understand now,
but afterward you will understand."

JOHN 13:7, ESV

The third week of July each year is a tricky one for me. I often find myself stuck and restless.

After suffering a miscarriage with our first pregnancy, we kept our second pregnancy quiet for months. But at 22 weeks with triplets, there comes a point where you can't stay silent anymore. In the third week of July, after celebrating our wedding anniversary, we told our friends we were having three boys. A week later, they were with Jesus.

That week's hard pivot from celebration to despair felt too much to bear. We had announced our three miracles sons to friends and family. We then immediately had to tell those same people that we lost the boys—all while congratulatory messages were still coming in. Why God allowed this to happen this way was such a mystery to me. It still is.

For some reason, the anniversary of the week in between is harder sometimes than the actual day. I still wonder why God even had us experience all the joys of this miracle pregnancy only to have it crushed. Then I think, even if only for a few days, our sons deserved to be celebrated.

I continue to wrestle with the grief of that week. And this doesn't disappear because of the joy that followed with my daughters' births. I continually try to wrap my head around the tension of my lack of understanding now with the promise that there is a "but afterward." It is this very promise that keeps me moving forward in hope.

The same suffering that almost destroyed me introduced me to a God who stuck with me through it and is still here with me now.

God is here with you, too, friend. In a heavy but temporary world, God has promised us an eternity where all things are made new in the "but afterward."

As you meditate on the stepping stone of God's promise of making all things new and clear in eternity, I invite you to consider this:

T: Give God thanks for the gift of his son and the promise of an eternity where you will no longer wrestle.

H: Pray that the promise of "but afterward" gives you hope today as you rest in the tension of the brokenness on earth with the glory yet to come.

I: As you sit in this tension, ask God to help you trust him with what you do not understand today.

S: Can you surrender your heart to this promise today? Ask God to help you shift your gaze on eternity as you rest in him today.

For this, I prayed.

ONE DAY CLOSER

He will swallow up death forever; and the Lord God will
wipe away tears from all faces, and the reproach of
his people he will take away from all the earth, for the
Lord has spoken. It will be said on that day, "Behold,
this is our God; we have waited for him, that he might
save us. This is the Lord, we have waited for him; let us
be glad and rejoice in his salvation."

ISAIAH 25:8–9, ESV

My three favorite words in this passage are "on that day."

As previously shared, after we lost our sons, my husband planted peonies in our garden to honor their lives. Each year, after they finish blooming for the season, I get peonies delivered from around the country until they are done for good for the year, usually around November.

With each set of peonies, I write a note to myself that says, "One day closer."

Each year, with the last set of peonies for the season, I try to hang on to them for as long as possible. I appreciate them when they are broken and falling apart just as much as when they are in full bloom. I hang on now because after our sons passed away, I had one last chance to hold them, and I couldn't bring myself to do it. Deep down, I wish that I had.

It's hard to hold on to something you know you won't have forever. But each day, even as I watch the peonies fade away, I smile to myself because it is one day closer to forever, and all will be made new on that day.

> "For the Lord himself will come down from heaven with a commanding shout, with the voice of the archangel, and with the trumpet call of God. First, the believers who have died will rise from their graves. Then, together with them, we who are still alive and remain on the earth will be caught up in the clouds to meet the Lord in the air. Then we will be with the Lord forever."

1 THESSALONIANS 4:16–17, NLT

One day closer, and on that day - what an incredible promise!

We live in a hard but hopeful world. Even as we wait on forever, we rest in the abundance of the here and now. Because of eternity, the broken is made beautiful. And when grief breaks your spirit, God's love and his promise for that day hold together the fractured pieces of your heart.

I don't know where you find yourself today, my friend, but I pray you will embrace God's love. This love is forever unbroken. It expands with each breath you take, making room in your heart to appreciate new and different blessings here on earth that will bring you hope as you wait for that one sweet day.

As you meditate on the stepping stone of God's promise of eternity, I invite you to consider this:

T: Lord, we thank you for the promise that even today is one day closer.

H: I thank you, God, that because the grave is empty, we do not grieve without hope.

I: Even as I struggle with grief today, give me tangible reminders of your presence, Lord. Remind me that I am not alone.

S: As I try to hold on tightly to that which is temporary here on earth, help me to loosen my grip, exhale, and surrender the brokenness into your hands. Dear God, help me never to lose sight of eternity and the completeness of joy on that day.

For this, I prayed.

SIX:

STONE OF

OF

suffering

STONE OF SUFFERING

I don't like suffering.

Over the years, I have cringed at the passage, "Consider it pure joy, my brothers and sisters, whenever you face trials of many kinds, because you know that the testing of your faith produces perseverance." (James 1:2-3, NIV)

I don't know many people who consider their suffering "pure joy." Romans 5 tells us that this suffering and perseverance will lead to hope, and while I want to get to this hope, I would rather bypass the process often required to get there. I have spent many nights wondering how I place my trust in a God who allows me to suffer. Yet, on those same nights, I knew he was holding me.

Suffering is never the final stop.

It is a medium used to produce a change because our Father enters our suffering with us and transforms it into something beautiful.

I have become most intimately aware of God and his character in the middle of my deepest pain. In my suffering and weakest moments, I have heard God's voice, felt his love, and seen his strength. He sees us in our pain because he took on suffering for us.

Jesus suffered, and he suffered for us, and because of his suffering, our pain is never the end of the story. And that is the good news of the Gospel. In our darkest hour, he sits with us, and we can hear him whisper, "I see you, and I know." We can lean into his suffering as we "consider that the sufferings of this present time are not worth comparing with the glory that is to be revealed to us." (Romans 8:18, ESV)

When I stop to consider that even while suffering, God causes everything to work for our good and for his glory, I ask myself, "Is this suffering worth it for the good of someone else?" For me, the answer is not always a yes. I'm not always willing to go through struggle if I can't see where it will lead to my earthly gain. But I have realized that sometimes our struggles are for the one who needs to see God's presence and his glory in our story.

We all need to see someone who has triumphed not on the other side of pain but whose victory was the joy they found amid the darkness. We suffer in community; sometimes, our suffering leads to someone else's thanksgiving.

My ability to offer thanksgiving, to live hopeful in the midst of suffering, and to surrender to God's sovereignty is because I have seen others find the joy of the Lord in times of struggle.

In the same way, I pray your faith is lifted by the strength of those around you, a strength grounded in our weakness and the power resulting from his suffering.

The victory isn't always that we overcome on this side of eternity, but sometimes it is a pure joy that comes when we endure. As we suffer, we unite with him as he meets us with his presence, grace, power, and love.

As you meditate on the stepping stone of his suffering, I invite you to pray this with me:

T: Father, we thank you that we are not alone in our suffering. Thank you for sending your son, who is no stranger to pain, to suffer for us.

H: I thank you that because of your suffering, my current affliction is not my final destination because you have promised to transform my suffering into hope.

I: Even in my pain today, help me remember that you are right there with me and will get the glory.

S: Help me see you as I surrender, lean into your suffering, and find joy as I rest in your sovereignty.

For this, I prayed.

the sufferings of
this present time are
not worth comparing
with the glory
that is to be revealed
to us

romans 8:18

TREASURES IN THE DARKNESS

And I will give you treasures
hidden in the darkness – secret riches.
I will do this so you may know that I am the Lord,
the God of Israel, the one who calls you by name.

ISAIAH 45:3, NLT

Before our sons passed away, we had a miscarriage early into
our first pregnancy one year prior. After years of infertility and
five cycles of IVF, that was the first time we ever had a positive
pregnancy test. But within six short weeks, our hopes were crushed
by a phone call from the doctor. The growth numbers were not
good, and we were to expect a miscarriage in the following days.

I thought we would have a little more time to celebrate our sweet
baby in the shelter of my womb, but later that night, we lost our
first baby. We never confirmed the gender, but we knew our first
son would be named Gideon Isaiah.

I was angry that we never had a chance to share our joy with the
world. I wanted my baby to be seen and loved. But the Lord met
me and held me in the darkness. He showed me that while very
few people would know of the suffering we would experience,
Gideon Isaiah was and still is a gift and treasure hidden in the
darkness. A treasure seen and known by the Father above, and a
child he would call by name.

As we went into future IVF cycles, we held on to that positive
pregnancy test as one of our secret riches. It was a sign of the hope
of Jesus that would bring joy amid an impossible situation and the

assurance that he would meet us with his peace in future seasons of darkness.

In a world filled with brokenness, it is hard to see the goodness of the Lord in the depths of suffering. Only the Father can help us see the treasures hidden in pain and show us the most significant gift that originated in darkness, his Son Jesus.

As you meditate on the secrets hidden in times of suffering, I invite you to consider this:

T: Lord, we thank you that even in suffering, you gift us with treasures the world may not see or understand. Ask God to show you the secrets in your current season of struggle.

H: As you reflect, think of the hope of Jesus, our biggest treasure in the darkness. How does this hope help you trust God in this season?

I: Ask God to show you his light in your current circumstance. Pray this light will allow you to experience his peace.

S: Ask the Lord to help you rest in him and assure you that you are seen and loved and that even in this, he is still sovereign and good.

For this, I prayed.

BROKEN BLINDS

I could ask the darkness to hide me
and the light around me to become night –
but even in darkness, I cannot hide from you.

PSALM 139:11–12, NLT

As I write this, every set of blinds in our house is broken.

My daughter walks around breaking blinds. We used to go around and fix them, but at some point, we just gave up. Or perhaps we gave in—to the reality of the brokenness and the joy in the hands causing the breaking.

One morning, after she had broken some new blinds, I asked her why she continued to do this. She responded, "Because I wanted to let in the light, of course!"

Over the years, there have been many times when life has threatened to break me as I have struggled to keep it all together. When I wanted to give up, I wondered, what if I gave in instead?

What if I leaned into the promise of resurrection that was inherent in the suffering of Jesus?

What if I leaned into his promise to always carry me and my suffering?

What if I allowed myself to be broken in surrender to the one who is carrying me?

What if, in the breaking, I surrendered to his sovereignty instead of my suffering?

And, finally, what if being broken actually lets the light in?

I realized that over the years, hiding in the darkness consumed me to the degree that I gave up on the light shining through the brokenness.

Dear friend, even in this darkness, his light will find you. And that light may be the hope and miracle you need right now. Please don't give up. Give in and surrender to him and his promise to be your light, even in this current season of suffering.

As you meditate on this stepping stone and lean into the promise of his light born from his suffering, I invite you to consider this:

T: Lord, you promised that darkness and light are the same to you. Thank you for your light.

H: As you reflect on the light of Jesus, how does knowing that his light will find you even in the darkest pit give you hope?

I: In your darkness, ask the Lord to lead you to his light. Ask him to help you to not give up but to lean into him.

S: Ask God to help you surrender and to stop hiding from him in the darkness. Ask him to help you embrace his light that shines through every broken area of your life today.

For this, I prayed.

FOR THE ONE

We rejoice in our sufferings,
knowing that suffering produces endurance,
and endurance produces character,
and character produces hope,
and hope does not put us to shame,
because God's love has been poured
into our hearts through the Holy Spirit
who has been given to us.

ROMANS 5:3–5, ESV

As someone who has endured so much, I never thought I would "rejoice" in suffering. This passage of scripture is another one that has stumped me over the years.

When I was in the middle of my infertility struggle, I remember the Lord clearly speaking to me one day. He said, "What if this is for the one?" Over the years, while I never understood, I held on to the phrase "for the one."

After sharing portions of our journey more broadly, I began interacting with several women walking through seasons of endometriosis, infertility, or the grief of losing a child. I have stood with women as they have rejoiced in healing or the birth of their miracle child, and I have sat with women as they have mourned the loss of a child or grieved a life that is different than they imagined.

Then, the Lord reminded me of the phrase "for the one."

As Jesus passed a man who was blind from birth, people wondered whose sin led to the man's suffering. In response, Jesus says,

"Neither this man nor his parents sinned. This came about so that God's works might be displayed in him." (John 9:3, CSB)

If you are going through a tough time, friend, know this is not your fault. Terrible things happen to good people; sometimes, God desires to use us as vessels to display his glory as we rejoice in our suffering. But we are only able to rejoice as we look forward in hope.

As I sit with people in their darkness, I realize so much of my hope for others formed in previous seasons of my suffering. With each journey, my endurance was a little more than before, and as a result, my character and hope grew. And because of God's love, we do not hope in this world but in the unshakeable foundation of Jesus, who died and rose again to conquer suffering. Upon his foundation, we stand. Praise God!

We know that future trials in our lives are inevitable. I noticed that as I shared the hope of Jesus with others, my suffering also enabled me to receive the hope that I would need in future seasons of despair.

Sometimes, I looked in the mirror and realize I was "the one."

Dear friend, I don't know where you find yourself today, but it isn't easy to rejoice in your current season. Lean into my hope. I pray that as you do, you will not hear my voice but the voice of Jesus as he pours into your heart through the Holy Spirit and transforms your suffering into endurance, character, and hope for a brighter tomorrow.

As you meditate on this stepping stone and the transformation of your suffering into hope, I invite you to consider this:

T: Reflect on seasons when someone came alongside you in your suffering. Give God thanks for reminding you of his love in a difficult time.

H: How does the promise of hope help you today as you consider rejoicing in your suffering?

I: Ask God to help you to hear his voice as he meets you in your suffering. Ask him to send someone your way as a tangible sign that he is with you and will never leave you.

S: As you surrender to God in your current season, find a healthy community, if possible. Allow his love to wash over you through his people. Lean into the hope of others as you struggle to rejoice in your present circumstances.

For this, I prayed.

GOD SEES, GOD HEARS

Yahweh, you have heard the desires
of the humble and seen their hopes.
You will hear their cries
and encourage their hearts.

PSALM 10:17, TPT

When I struggled with excruciating pain from flares due to endometriosis, I could not do much around the house. Fortunately, we got an assistant to help us clean and cook periodically and it was such a big blessing.

One day in particular, I was in a lot of pain. It was also the only day that our assistant was late. Her ride never came, so my husband, who was on his way to run an errand, had to take a detour to pick her up. When she finally arrived, she walked in with a surprise. She brought me the most beautiful flowers from her garden.

Flowers always bring me joy, even when I am in pain. The thing is, the errand my husband was going on was to get me flowers.

She didn't know I needed cheering up, she didn't know I was having a tough day, and she didn't even know I liked flowers. She was waiting on a ride that never showed, and as she waited, the Lord had her pick up some flowers.

Even though she did not know, God knew. He heard my cries, saw my pain, and cared enough to encourage my heart in a time of suffering.

At the end of that day, though I was in pain, I had a clean home, dinner, flowers, and, best of all, hope.

The Lord hears you, friend. You are not alone in your suffering. God has listened to your cries and seen your tears. I pray he will send you a tangible sign encouraging your heart today.

As you meditate on this stepping stone and the God who sees and hears you in your suffering, I invite you to consider this:

T: Reflect on a time when you have received an unexpected phone call, visit, or other physical display of his goodness during a difficult season. Thank God for his encouragement.

H: How does knowing God sees your hopes help you keep hoping and not give up in your season of despair?

I: Even now, ask God to encourage you in your dry season. Ask him to refresh you with his Spirit.

S: As you surrender, I encourage you to hope once more. God sees you. He hears you. He is for you.

For this, I prayed.

GREAT POWER

We now have this light shining in our hearts, but we
ourselves are like fragile clay jars containing this great
treasure. This makes it clear that our great power
is from God, not from ourselves. We are pressed on
every side by troubles, but we are not crushed. We are
perplexed, but not driven to despair. We are hunted
down, but never abandoned by God. We get knocked
down, but we are not destroyed.

2 CORINTHIANS 4:7–9, NLT

As you read this passage, I encourage you to read all of Chapter 4
in the book of 2 Corinthians. I believe the word of the Lord brings
healing, clarity, encouragement, light, and hope in our suffering.
And I trust the word of God to speak to you in a way only he can.

Meditate on these words from your Father. Replace the "we" with
"I" and the "our" with "my" and make it personal.

Many of us grew up thinking we would get it done if we tried
hard enough. But what happens when your strength is not enough
to stop the suffering? How does this suppress our hope and our
thanksgiving?

We cannot put limits on God
that depend on our own power.

So many people think I am so strong after all I have been through.
Trust me, I do not have that kind of endurance. I only survive

and find joy because I am a fragile piece of clay that is broken and bruised but filled to overflowing with the power of God. And you, my friend, have that same power living inside of you. Don't give up!

As you meditate on this stepping stone and the God who fills you with power in your suffering, I invite you to consider this:

T: Give the Lord thanks for his strength that is being made perfect in your weakness. Consider that even now, he is causing your broken heart to overflow with a great power that only comes from him.

H: Give God thanks for the hope that you are never abandoned or consumed. Thank him for the promise that you will rise with him even as you share in the suffering of Jesus.

I: Even now, in your pain, ask God to help you to keep believing and trusting in him. Ask him to keep your gaze fixed on what is unseen as you remain focused on the glory that will be revealed even in this season of suffering.

S: As you surrender, pray that your heart will be encouraged with the knowledge that even as this crushing did not destroy your sisters in the faith, you will not be overwhelmed. God will not leave you alone. Ask him to help you to keep trusting even when it doesn't make sense. Pray for the strength to rest in his sovereignty and his overwhelming peace.

For this, I prayed.

SEVEN:

STONE
OF
Covenant

STONE OF COVENANT

After four years of courtship, on May 17, 2003, Andrew asked me to be his wife. I remember the day clearly because that week, he had visited for the first time since I moved to the United States. I planned quite the itinerary, but we had a huge disagreement that morning.

I stepped away for some time alone to reflect on our relationship, and shortly after, there was a knock at the door. I don't remember much of what Andrew said, but he presented me with an engagement ring and a promise. He promised to remain committed to me and us, even in the worst of times. I remember thinking, this is not the romantic engagement I imagined. But years later, I realized that moment was a precursor to my husband's commitment every day since that morning.

Our marriage has not been a fairytale. We have had sickness before we had health, worse before we had better, and sorrow before gladness. But in the worst of times, he chose to stay, he chose to love, and he chose to fight for us. It's easy to decide to love amidst the beauty and glamor of young love and marriage, but when you choose to love every day in the good and the bad, it's called "covenant love." A covenant is the foundation that allows you to choose love even when you don't feel like it.

When we got married, we never intended to walk the journey of pain that we have endured. But God has continued to strengthen us as a couple, and in Andrew, he deposited the qualities of a compassionate, gentle, yet strong, decisive leader. With my husband, God has gifted me the memorial stone of a covenant.

A covenant exists so that love can continue to grow, even when your spouse is seemingly unlovable. Covenant chooses consistency over feelings and chooses love without limits. Our marriage faithfully reminds me that we serve a God who keeps his covenants with us.

> "I will not violate my covenant or
> alter what my lips have uttered."
>
> **PSALM 89:34, ESV**

We weren't sure how the story of our marriage would unfold amid the darkness. Still, our all-knowing God answered prayers that we never even prayed in his ultimate kindness, divine wisdom, perfect timing, and unparalleled goodness. God's plans truly exceeded our dreams.

Looking back, I realize that it wasn't just the result that was an answer to prayer. The process was an answered prayer as well. God has always had a purpose for our marriage, which the enemy has tried extremely hard to destroy, but the stone of covenant love has continued to prevail.

As with marriage, the Christian journey is both beautiful and challenging. We figure out how to maneuver through some pretty hard stuff with joy, even when we don't understand or agree with the ways of life. But dear friend, at all times, I pray that our marriages and our walks with God bear fruit that makes it impossible for anyone to doubt the covenant of love that God has promised.

> "Know therefore that the Lord your God is God; He
> is the faithful God, keeping his covenant of love to a
> thousand generations."
>
> **DEUTERONOMY 7:9**

As you meditate on the stepping stone of his covenant, I invite you to consider this:

T: Thank God for keeping his covenant of love to us in the good and bad times. Reflect on his love, not as something you have to earn but something that has been given freely to you.

H: As you reflect on this covenant, how does it give you hope in seasons of darkness? Does it help you trust that God is with you at all times, in all things?

I: Even now, ask God to send you relationships that show you a glimmer of your covenant relationship with your heavenly Father.

S: How does this covenant relationship with God encourage you as you surrender to him and rest in his sovereignty?

For this, I prayed.

He is the faithful god, keeping His covenant of love to a thousand generations.

Deuteronomy 7:9

UNSHAKEABLE PEACE

Though the mountains be shaken and the hills be removed, yet my unfailing love for you will not be shaken nor my covenant of peace be removed, says the Lord who has compassion on you.

ISAIAH 54:10, NIV

I question why I am joyful, even after all the struggles I have endured. But after living a life filled with physical pain, losing my children, struggling financially, emotionally, and spiritually, and fighting for my marriage, one thing has remained constant. My Redeemer lives, and he has never let me go.

God has indeed been with me in the fire, and his covenant of peace, established in advance, continues to change the tragedy of my story into a hopeful one of redemption and restoration.

The best part of my story is that God is in it, and he is stronger than the challenges. And because he lives, the story you see in me is never the end. It is always the beginning. Every day brings new mercies and the beginning of a new chapter.

Dear friend, I do not know your story or the valley where you may find yourself today, but I want to encourage you with this: *God is a mighty covenant partner, willing and able to take the broken pieces in your life and hold them together with unshakeable peace.*

Because of this covenant, God's love, compassion, and peace are steadfast and immovable even as the seasons of struggle come. Rest in this promise, my friend.

As you meditate on the stepping stone of his covenant of peace, I invite you to consider this:

T: Thank God for his covenant of peace even when everything around us crumbles.

H: How does God's covenant of peace during your struggle give you hope for redemption, restoration, and rest in your own story?

I: Even now, invite God into your heart and your story. Let your guard down. You can trust him to fill you with his peace.

S: How does God's peace allow you to rest in him? Are you breathing a little easier? Inhale his peace and exhale your worries as you surrender today.

For this, I prayed.

LET HIM LEAD

But among you it will be different. Whoever wants to be a leader among you must be your servant, and whoever wants to be first among you must become your slave. For even the Son of Man came not to be served but to give his life as a ransom for many.

MATTHEW 20:26–28, NLT

Growing up, I loved to dance. As a family, we would dance in our living rooms, car, and store—we didn't even need music to start dancing. As Andrew and I started planning our wedding, the thing I was most looking forward to was our first dance. But there was one problem: Andrew does not like to dance. Not even a little bit. As a compromise, I picked one of the shortest love songs I could find and promised him just one dance.

Over the years, I have asked him a few times to dance with me, and he obliges me, but I know not to ask him in public. However, he gifted me dance lessons for our fifteenth wedding anniversary for us both. I was thrilled. I looked forward to being able to lead as I helped him learn these new styles of dance—until I realized that in the world of ballroom dance, he is supposed to lead, and I am supposed to follow.

As we started lessons, we couldn't get the hang of it. It was challenging for Andrew to lead in an area where I was naturally stronger, and I struggled to follow his lead. It was hard to submit to his leadership because I did not realize he was serving me in his choosing to follow an uncomfortable path. While the initial lessons were a struggle for both of us, as I learned to follow, I embraced the vision of where he was leading me.

We may not have perfected the art of ballroom dance, but we grew in love, respect, and trust for one another. And that has spilled over into other areas of our marriage.

While the world tends to applaud those at the top of their game, the kingdom views the leader as the one who serves. God's covenant of leadership is most evident in how he sacrificed and uncomfortably served us, his children.

Sometimes, it is hard to surrender our plans fully, especially when we need to change direction or put down something that is going well. But as we submit to him, we can entrust our lives to the leadership of the only One who has paid the ultimate price—the life of his son Jesus.

As you meditate on the stepping stone of his covenant of leadership, I invite you to consider this:

T: Give God thanks that you do not have to figure out life in this world on your own. Reflect on the knowledge that you have Christ as a leader who came to edify his children through the act of service.

H: How does God's leadership covenant help you keep hoping when nothing goes according to plan? Can you trust that he is leading you even when you can't see where you may be going?

I: In your journey, take a moment to reflect on if there is anyone in your community you can serve today. Where can you show up for someone, even in your struggle?

S: I want to encourage you to surrender to God's guidance today. It is hard to follow a path that leads to an unknown destination, but

I promise a kind Father who sees and knows every way you take is leading. You can trust him today.

For this, I prayed.

HE CALLS YOU FRIEND

Then Jonathan made a covenant with David,
and Jonathan loved him as his own soul.

1 SAMUEL 18:3, ESV

We had some overripe bananas on the counter when I visited home for the holidays. As they were about to be thrown away, I grabbed them to do what my grandma would do—make banana bread.

My parents do not bake and have no utensils or baking pans—except for one wonky tin. It was pretty bent out of shape. When they cleared out my grandma's house, this was the only baking tin left, so my dad held on to it. She was the baker in our family, and the tin was at least 70 years old at the time. Each year, she would bake dozens of breads, pies, and cakes for the entire family, the neighborhood, and all our friends. Everyone wanted something from her kitchen.

As I washed out the tin, I noticed an inscription on the bottom: BAIR. Mrs. Bair was her neighbor and a dear friend. My grandmother baked so much that she never had enough tins, so she would send us to borrow tins from her neighbor. Mrs. Bair passed away years before my grandmother, but my grandmother still held on to this borrowed tin. It represented decades of friendship.

My grandma passed away shortly after she celebrated her 100th birthday, and now I am baking for my family and friends in that same tin. Each time I use it, I never know how my baking will turn out as it is so old and thin. But much like the covenant friendship between my grandma and her neighbor, the pan keeps holding up. It continues to withstand the test of time. And while it bends under the heat, it does not break.

Covenant friendship is such a gift from God. As we encounter these friendships here on earth, of them all, Jesus is the best. He is a great and faithful friend who chases after you with his goodness, mercy, and love. It is filled with truth as he confides in us through his word.

> "Now you are my friends, since I have told you everything the Father told me. You didn't choose me, I chose you."
>
> **JOHN 15:15–16, NLT**

No matter what you may face today, remember that Jesus loves you. Jesus chose you. Jesus calls you friend.

As you meditate on the stepping stone of his covenant of friendship, I invite you to consider this:

T: Take a moment to give God thanks for being your friend. As you do this, reflect on the friendships he has sent you, which have helped shape your life thus far.

H: How does knowing that your friendship will not break despite the trials give you hope to keep going?

I: Share this gift of friendship with someone else by being a friend today.

S: How can you rest in the love of Jesus today, knowing that no matter what, his friendship will always remain?

For this, I prayed.

ESTABLISHED FOREVER

You have said, "I have made a covenant with
my chosen one; I have sworn to David my
servant, I will establish your offspring forever,
and build your throne for all generations."

PSALM 89:3-4, ESV

God reminds David of the earlier generational covenant he established in the above verse. However, when David gets to verse 46 in that same chapter, he cries to God, asking him, "How long will you hide yourself forever?"

Like David, our children aren't good at waiting before complaining, "How much longer?" They are quick to point out if they think we have not kept our promises to them. And the truth is, we are no different.

We quickly forget that God doesn't only make covenants. He keeps covenants.

Oftentimes, it appears as if God has not kept his promises, and we struggle to rest in generational covenants. But as we follow God, our trust in him must be greater than our desire for an immediate answer to our problems.

Ultimately, God kept his promise to David through the birth of Jesus. And because of Jesus, God honors that promise to us, his children, and all future generations.

Sometimes, it helps me remember that God is not just any father. He is my Daddy, the one who loves me unconditionally. And even as I desire to work to set a foundation for my children to succeed, how much more will my Daddy take care of me? And my friend, he will take care of you too.

As you meditate on the stepping stone of his generational covenants, I invite you to consider this:

T: Give God thanks for being an awesome Dad! Reflect on what it means to have a Father who loves and cares for you and seeks to provide for you and your future generations.

H: How does the reminder that God has kept his generational covenants through the gift of Jesus give you hope that he will keep his promises concerning you?

I: As you reflect on this hope, ask God to reveal himself to you so you can continue to wait on him when you get weary.

S: Write these verses from Psalm 89 on the tablet of your heart and refer to it even as you surrender your plans to him, even when you inevitably cry, "How long?" Not only will you be established, but God promises to establish and build up all those connected to you. And that, my friend, is good news.

For this, I prayed.

A BETTER COVENANT

The Lord has sworn and will not change his mind,
"You are a priest forever." This makes Jesus the
guarantor of a better covenant.

HEBREWS 7:21-22, ESV

Over the years, my health prevented me from doing much physical activity with my daughters. There were times when I would make promises and have to apologize because I could not keep my promise. But their dad always kept his promises.

I noticed that one day, they didn't ask me as much anymore. Anytime they wanted anything, they would run to their dad. The truth was Daddy's promises were more guaranteed than mine.

While it was a hard pill to swallow, I embraced the depth of the relationship that my husband built with our daughters. I often joke that I am praying for their future husbands in advance because the bar has been set so high. He is their best friend, and I am okay with that.

But one day, he had to delay a promise to them. When they questioned him, he responded, "Because Daddy is human, and ultimately, Jesus is the only one who will never break a promise."

Jesus is a much better promise-keeper than man will ever be. Because of his sacrifice, he became the guarantor of a better covenant—one that lasts into eternity.

Occasionally, we get frustrated because we depend on a local priest or family and friends to do things only Jesus can do. He is the only one who saves, restores, redeems, and intercedes for us with his Father. Inevitably, we will mess up, but Jesus gets it right every time.

As you meditate on the stepping stone of Jesus, the guarantor of a better covenant, I invite you to consider the following prayer:

T: Father, thank you for the gift of your son—a gift that not only intercedes on our behalf but grants us access to you.

H: Help us keep our eyes fixed on you, our one true hope, and not dwell on the disappointments of earthly priests, family, or friends.

I: We ask that you forgive us for the times we turned our back on you, thinking you were like everyone else. Help us remain faithful, believe in you, and allow your Holy Spirit to dwell in us.

S: I surrender my will, my thoughts, and the desires of my flesh to you. Help me receive the acceptance and forgiveness you so freely give, and then extend this same forgiveness and grace to others.

For this, I prayed.

EIGHT:

STONE
OF
presence

STONE OF PRESENCE

In 2013, I gave birth to three sons, Noah, Caleb, and Micah. After experiencing only minutes of life here on earth, they are now dancing, breathing, and living fully in eternity with Jesus.

In the weeks and months following their transition from death to eternal life, the two biggest lessons their lives taught me were that God is always with me and God is good to me. Because living here on earth in the presence of a good God is the only way I could survive living without them.

Losing my sons broke me in a way I never thought possible. They were such a miracle, and after waiting for so long with the hope of becoming parents, in a matter of days, all our dreams vanished as we left the hospital with empty arms and crushed hearts.

For days, I refused visitors, even turning away my family, as the pain was too much to bear. It was easier to be alone, but even in this, God pursued me, he met me, and he held me. In those moments, I became intimately close to the character of God, Emmanuel, "God with us."

Even as I struggled with God and the reality that my sons had slipped out of my hands, I had to trust that they were held ever so tightly in his. I believed they were forever with him, and I realized that as long as he was with me, I would forever be close to my sons. And just as Emmanuel will forever hold and never leave them, he will also hold us.

One day in particular, I locked myself in the bathroom as I cried uncontrollably on the floor. I refused to even let my husband in. Then suddenly, I heard someone sit on the other side of the door and saw a gentle hand slip underneath. My friend Zara had traveled from out of state to see me. She sat on the floor for hours as I cried. And with her hand in the same spot, she prayed and cried. At that moment, when I thought God had abandoned me, he met me there, through my friend, on the bathroom floor.

In the darkness, God never left. He entered in, and he stayed. And even now, when the waves of grief suddenly rise, I remember God is still here.

> "And I will lead the blind in a way that they do not know, in paths that they have not known I will guide them. I will turn the darkness before them into light, the rough places into level ground. These are the things I do, and I do not forsake them."

ISAIAH 42:16, ESV

Dear friend, I don't know where you find yourself today. You may have dreams that didn't go the way you planned. You may be in a dark place as something you desperately wanted has slipped away. I want to encourage you that God sees you and has not abandoned you, and even in this story, the truth that he is with you on your bathroom floor of brokenness proves that God is still good. My prayer for you is that you will feel Jesus near you today.

As you meditate on the stepping stone of God's presence, I invite you to join me in this prayer:

T: Lord, I thank you for always pursuing me in all things. Thank you for never abandoning me. Thank you for making sure I am never alone.

H: Help me believe in your promise to turn all darkness into light one day. Help me always to remember the hope of eternity that is in you.

I: Lord, in my pain, help me to trust that even when my dreams are out of my hands, they are securely held and protected in yours.

S: Help me always to surrender, even when my heart is breaking. Lead and guide me by your mighty hand.

For this, I prayed.

and surely i am
with you always
to the very end
of the age

matthew 28:20

STAND STILL

And there was the cloud and the darkness. And it lit up
the night without one coming near the other all night.
Then Moses stretched out his hand over the sea, and the
Lord drove the sea back by a strong east wind all night
and made the sea dry land, and the waters were divided.

EXODUS 14:20-21, ESV

There are times when things seem like they are going so well, and
then suddenly, just as you start declaring victory, you are again on
the run from the brokenness and pain in this world. For a minute,
you think you have escaped the suffering. Then you realize the
darkness is chasing you once again, and it is more than you can
bear.

Often, our family felt chased by calamity as we somehow found
a way to survive infertility and grief, then subsequently battling
a chronic illness that had me bedridden. After experiencing
miraculous healing, we began learning to maneuver the new
world of autism. Then, as we started settling into our new normal,
we battled financial challenges and new health scares. In these
moments, it is easy to forget that God has given you victory before,
and you start to wonder, "God, where are you? Do you see what's
going on here?"

In Exodus 14:10, as Pharaoh and the Egyptians got closer to the Israelites, they became terrified. Yet, Moses was confident in the Lord's ability to deliver them, even in the wilderness. As I reflected on Moses' faith in the Lord, I remember that in Exodus 3, Moses encountered the Lord. In Exodus 3:7, the Lord tells Moses that he has seen the sufferings of his people, heard their cries, and will deliver them. This assurance lifted Moses's faith, and he knew that no matter the circumstance, the Lord would bring deliverance to his people.

As I have struggled from one season to the next, this same assurance has given me hope that God sees me, hears my cries, and will deliver me. And my friend, he will deliver you, too. Even in this, God is with you and will not leave you alone.

As with the Israelites, when God was with them and led them forward in the darkness, God will stay with you, dear friend, and guide you through. Even though you cannot see, God has seen and heard you, and he is standing with you and ready to part the raging waters on your behalf.

Fear not, my friend. Stand still and watch the Lord work it all out for you today.

As you meditate on the stepping stone of God's presence that leads you even in darkness, I invite you to consider this:

T: Give thanks to God for his continual presence and how he leads and guides you even in the darkness.

H: As you reflect on God's presence leading you in darkness, how does the assurance that God sees your suffering, hears your cries, and promises to deliver you give you hope in your current season?

I: Even while suffering, ask God to help you not to be bitter in the wilderness. Ask him to show you a tangible sign that his pillar of cloud is with you and will protect you from any pain currently chasing you.

S: Dear friend, I want to invite you to stand still in surrender to the Lord today. Rest in his presence and his promise that he will fight for you and deliver you.

For this, I prayed.

EVEN HERE

I can never escape your Spirit! I can never get
away from your presence! If I go up to heaven, you
are there; if I go down to the grave, you are there.
If I ride the wings of the morning, if I dwell by the
farthest oceans, even there your hand will guide
me, and your strength will support me.

PSALM 139:7–10, NLT

We have cameras in our daughters' bedroom. Not only can we see
what's going on in the room, but we can speak to them as well.
While they know the cameras exist, they often forget that we can
see them and that even though we may not be right next to them,
we can still provide guidance.

I remember when I was extremely sick and couldn't get out of bed.
On that day in particular, Andrew had gone to run errands, and I
was home with the kids. While he was gone, my daughters were
playing in their room when I suddenly heard crying. There was
a toy they couldn't find, and for them, this was a huge problem.
When I turned on the monitor, I couldn't get their attention
because they wouldn't calm down long enough to hear me calling
them.

While they cried, I scanned the room for the toy and quickly found
it. I waited until they got tired of crying, and then I called out to
them and guided them to what they desired. It was there all along.
I was there all along.

They were so frustrated by their circumstances and the fact they couldn't immediately see me running to their aid that they forgot I was still there and could still see and hear them. And that's how it is with us sometimes as children of God.

When faced with struggles, if we don't always get a quick response to our problems, *we forget that our pain is not a measure of God's presence.*

God has not left you, my friend. Even in your lowest valleys, God sees you, he hears you, he is waiting to guide you, and he will strengthen you with his mighty hand. I invite you to trust that even when you can't see God, he is near and working on your behalf.

As you meditate on the stepping stone of God's presence that exists even when you can't see or feel him, I invite you to consider this:

T: Give thanks to God for a time when you have felt his tangible presence. How does that help you trust him when you may not be able to see him in that moment?

H: As you reflect on God's presence that is always near, how can you rest in the constant nature of his character, and how does that give you hope in your current season of waiting?

I: In your current circumstance, ask God to help you trust that he is near. Ask a friend to pray with you concerning any doubts in your mind and heart if you can. Allow this truth to strengthen you as you wait on him.

S: Dear friend, I know you may be tired. I want to invite you to rest in the arms of Jesus. As you surrender to him, I pray that you will hear him whisper, as if he has been watching you on a camera all along, "I see you. I hear you. I am here with you. You are not alone."

For this, I prayed.

HOLD MY HAND

Then I realized that my heart was bitter, and I was all
torn up inside. I was so foolish and ignorant – I must
have seemed like a senseless animal to you. Yet I still
belong to you; you hold my right hand.

PSALM 73:21-23, NLT

Anyone who knows my husband will tell you he doesn't talk much.
As a result, communication was a big struggle for us early in our
marriage because I am notorious for telling you exactly how I
feel all the time, whether you like it or not, and usually, he didn't
respond. He would sit there, holding my hand.

When I was depressed, hiding in the closet or under the bed
crying, he wouldn't say anything. Instead, he would sit beside me
and hold my hand.

Whether we were walking through the grief of losing our sons
or celebrating the birth of our daughters, he was just not a very
expressive person. But he always held my hand.

It took me a long time to realize that the consistency of his
presence said so much more than his words ever could. Reflecting
on how I feel every time he holds my hand, I realize I never want
to take the feeling of constant safety, comfort, and love for granted.

There are times when it feels like God is silent, and as a result, our
hearts may grow bitter. We are confused, frustrated, and even angry
because we keep crying out to him, wondering if he is listening.
But even when we can't hear him, I want to encourage you in the
truth that you still belong to him, and he is holding your hand.

God is not far away from you.
He is right here, right now.

You can find comfort, guidance, safety, peace, and love in his hands. He longs for you, his beloved child, to trust in his hands today, even if you can't hear his voice.

As you meditate on the stepping stone of God's presence as he comes alongside you and holds your hand, I invite you to consider this:

T: I want to encourage you to thank your Heavenly Father for his presence even when you are bitter and forget his goodness. Give God thanks that he doesn't leave and continues to hold your hand.

H: As you reflect on God's presence, how does this assurance inspire you to hope as you think about the next time you may feel overwhelmed or despairing?

I: Amid your current circumstance, ask God to help you trust that he is near. Ask him to help your doubts and your unbelief.

S: As you surrender to God today, I want to invite you to close your eyes, take a few deep breaths, and imagine that your Heavenly Father is sitting right beside you. Now imagine him holding your hand as he whispers, "Keep going. I am so proud of you."

For this, I prayed.

BROKENHEARTED

The Lord is near to the brokenhearted
and saves the crushed in spirit.

PSALM 34:18, ESV

We were filled with hope when we entered the hospital in premature labor with our sons. Our faith was high after years of infertility, miscarriage, and waiting. We were confident that there was no way God had brought us this far for us to walk away empty-handed.

We came home from the hospital with broken hearts and a blue box.

Five years later, when we finally dared to open the blue box, we found the clothes they wore and a few blankets and pictures the nurses packaged to help us remember their short lives here on earth. I hoped that looking through the box would somehow fill the holes in my heart, but I realized that even with time, my heart has not felt any less broken. At some point, I stopped trying to put the pieces back together and gave in to the reality of my broken heart. And with each passing day, I felt Jesus increasingly near, just as he promised.

We live in a fallen world with suffering that leads to broken hearts. Unfortunately, this is a guarantee. Whether it's the loss of a friendship, the death of a loved one, or a crushed dream, it's hard to navigate through the grief of a spirit crushed with disappointment and pain. But praise God that while we may feel alone, God does not turn his back on our suffering; instead, he comes closer.

God is not only present in our seasons of pain; He draws near. He is not afraid to enter the messy parts of our lives. God is near to our losses, near to our unfulfilled dreams, and near to our broken hearts. In the darkness, he sits with us and holds us close. And the very nature of his presence saves and rescues us when we are crushed in spirit.

Receive God's love and nearness today, my friend. Allow him to draw close to you and rescue you as he holds on tightly to all the broken pieces of your heart.

As you meditate on the stepping stone of God's presence as he comes close to you in your pain, I invite you to consider this:

T: Thank God for hearing all our cries and coming close to us in our pain. I encourage you to imagine your Father is near you and tell him, "Thank you for coming!"

H: As you thank God for his presence, how does knowing he will never turn his back on any messes in your life restore your hope in him? Rest in the assurance that you will never be alone.

I: Even now, cry to God regarding whatever is crushing your spirit. Your Heavenly Father is close to you. You can find comfort in his embrace.

S: As you surrender the pieces of your broken heart to God, I invite you to try trusting him again. Trust that he will carry you, rescue you, and fill your heart with his love.

For this, I prayed.

WITH YOU ALWAYS

And surely I am with you always,
to the very end of the age.

MATTHEW 28:20, NIV

Grief lingers.

Many people say after being blessed with our daughters, we shouldn't still grieve the way we do. Others have said that we should move on. They pray that we never remember the pain. But that is the opposite of my prayer.

I pray that while we may move forward, we never move on. I pray that we never forget. I pray that as our grief lingers, it will continuously remind us of our love for our sons. A love that will never grow cold, a love that will never die. I pray we will never forget the God who met us in our pain and carried us. I pray that we will never forget that the same God dancing with our sons is sitting with us even now. He has promised to be with us always. We trust his promise.

Their deaths changed me. I will forever be different but hopeful. I never want to forget to keep living a life that reflects the lessons I learned from their death. Because even as the death of our sons was the most painful thing that has happened to us, it was not the most significant thing. The ultimate lesson we learned is God showed up and did the miraculous. That miracle is found not on the other side of pain but in the middle.

God held my heart together then and keeps holding my heart in the midst of all that lingers.

136

I don't think I will ever be on the other side of pain until the day I hold my sons in my arms again. But each day that I don't forget, I can live a life filled with joy, even as I long for my sons, because God is with me always until the very end of the age.

And God is with you, too, my friend. He was with you yesterday, he is with you today, and of a certainty, he will be with you tomorrow.

God has promised you that his presence in your life is a constant. I pray that you allow him to keep your eyes open to see his presence and walk in it because his presence brings joy. (Psalm 16:11)

Grief lingers, but so does the presence of God. I'm sure of it. May his presence today bring you hope, peace, and joy.

As you meditate on the stepping stone of God's constant presence, I invite you to consider this:

T: Thank God for his constant presence with you always. Praise him for his promise that even in the unknown, he has been there, he is there, and he will always be there.

H: How does the assurance of God's presence in your tomorrow encourage you and give you hope?

I: During your pain, ask God to reveal his presence to you. Ask him to fill you with his grace, strength, and peace for today and hope for tomorrow.

S: As you surrender to God today, allow your worries to be the foundation of your prayers. As you lean into his presence, ask him to trade your doubts for his joy!

For this, I prayed.

NINE:

STONE
OF
miracles

STONE OF MIRACLES

I write this stepping stone on miracles from the perspective of someone who has experienced multiple miracles in my lifetime.

Fortunately or unfortunately, on more than one occasion, I have received a change in my circumstances that the things of this world cannot explain. I use the word, unfortunately, because while many of us desire the miraculous, it is tough to be in a position where you need God's intervention to change an impossible situation.

As a family, we have witnessed the Lord's kindness through our daughters' miraculous birth. Doctors cannot explain how I am still alive after multiple life-threatening medical emergencies. And we have seen my mother come back from the brink of death. We have often said it felt like our miracles needed a miracle, and they did. Because the miracle we needed wasn't a change in our circumstances, the miracle was and always is Jesus.

I spent many years wanting to be healthy, wanting the perfect baby and the perfect marriage through every trial thrown our way. When we got pregnant with our sons, I thought we were seeing the manifestation of the miracle I desperately wanted. So, when we lost them, I wondered if God was indeed a God of miracles.

As Jesus took hold of my fragile heart and filled the holes with himself, I realized that after all these years of desiring the gift, the miracle I truly needed was the Giver.

"Jesus replied, 'If you only knew the gift God has for you and who you are speaking to, you would ask me, and I would give you living water.' 'But sir, you don't have a rope or a bucket,' she said, 'and this well is very deep. Where would you get this living water? And besides, do you think you're greater than our ancestor Jacob, who gave us this well? How can you offer better water than he and his sons and his animals enjoyed?' Jesus replied, 'Anyone who drinks this water will soon become thirsty again. But those who drink the water I give will never be thirsty again. It becomes a fresh, bubbling spring within them, giving them eternal life.'"

JOHN 4:10–14, NLT

Dear friend, the miracle is Jesus!

If you are in the midst of darkness or a season of waiting, I want to encourage you that the miracle you are searching for is Jesus. He is the only one who can grant you the desires of your heart and the peace you need when things don't work out as planned. And this miracle is a gift that keeps on giving. With Jesus, you will always have more than enough!

As you meditate on the stepping stone of his miracles, I invite you to join me in the following prayer:

T: Lord, thank you for what you have done in my life and for who you are. I thank you for the miracle of Jesus and the truth that this gift is the only thing that will fill our thirsty hearts.

H: Help us to always put our trust in you, Lord. Help us accept your love and assurance of peace and joy, and let this be the foundation of our hope.

I: Even in this current season of struggle, help us to keep our eyes fixed on you. Help us always to seek the Giver above the gift.

S: And as we surrender to you today, we declare that Lord, you are more than enough. We declare that we will rest in you even if things do not go according to our plans. We know everything we desire, we find in you.

For this, I prayed.

i remain confident
of this: i will see the
goodness of the
lord in the land
of the living

psalm 27:13

IN THE WAITING

For in this hope we were saved. Now hope that is seen is not hope. For who hopes for what he sees? But if we hope for what we do not see, we wait for it with patience.

ROMANS 8:24–25, ESV

There is a papaya tree at my childhood home in Jamaica. For 29 years, nobody had seen any fruit, and since nobody in my family had intentionally planted it, we all thought it was just an eyesore of weeds that needed uprooting.

Then, one day, somebody started watering the tree. And even though there was no sign of life, they kept waiting and watering, hoping for a future miracle they could not yet see. They watered the tree for years with no visible signs of what was to come, especially since the waterer tended something they had not planted.

And as they waited, God was working. He wasn't just doing something in the soil but also in the hearts of the ones watering the soil. Then suddenly, after living in the house for 29 years, we were stunned to find small papayas growing on the tree.

While the discovery blew our minds, it also encouraged our hearts as we thought of the gift of hope and patience we received while waiting. Our entire Christian journey embodies a posture of waiting on the future glory God will reveal to us in eternity. We do ourselves a disservice when we only focus on the miracle. Sometimes, the miracle is in the waiting and the way God uses it to grow our faith in him and increase our hunger for the day we see Jesus face to face.

Dear friend, I don't know what miracle you may seek, but I encourage you that your dream may be dormant. Keep watering. Even if you only do it routinely as you wait, I pray that you will allow God to use this time to build your faith.

Even as we keep praying, watering, and hoping in the waiting, our hopes rise as we depend entirely on God. Perhaps the miracle in our waiting is found when we surrender to him and his plans.

As you meditate on the stepping stone of his miracles in the waiting, I invite you to consider this:

T: Give God thanks for his promise, as in Ecclesiastes 3:11. He makes all things beautiful in their time. Give him thanks that even while you wait, he works miracles in and through you.

H: As you reflect on the truth that God is allowing a miracle in your heart even as you wait on him, how does this increase your hope? How does this increase your faith?

I: As you wait on God today, ask him to open your eyes to what is unseen. Ask him to remove your doubts and increase your patience while waiting on him.

S: I invite you to pray that you will fully depend on God in surrender today. Pray that he helps you live each day, even as you wait, with the perspective of the future glory you will see when Jesus returns.

For this, I prayed.

MY EYES HAVE SEEN

He alone is your God, the only one who is worthy
of your praise, the one who has done these mighty
miracles that you have seen with your own eyes.

DEUTERONOMY 10:21, NLT

Out of nowhere, my daughter asked me one day, "Mommy, what is a miracle?"

I told her a miracle is when something good happens that you can't explain, something you could never do by yourself. And I went on to tell her how the doctors said we would never have babies, but God gave them to us as gifts. I explained to her that she and her sister are our miracles.

She responded, "Well, Mommy, you are a miracle too. Remember when you were really sick, and then you weren't sick anymore? You were in bed all the time, and now you can finally play with us!"

With tears in my eyes, I told her how God provided so many miracles in our family, and she exclaimed, "Mommy, I believe in miracles!"

I have shared about the miraculous birth of our daughters multiple times. On occasion, someone would ask why I kept repeating the same story. The truth is, I never get tired of sharing what God has done in our lives. I never want it to become familiar or ordinary. And I pray that my daughters always believe the same power that raised Jesus from the dead works in their lives today. God has done mighty miracles I have seen with my own eyes, and I pray my girls always believe!

I don't know the prayer on your heart today, and I don't see the outcome of your story, but I believe. I believe God hears your cries, has seen your tears, and can make the impossible a reality in your life as he uses your story for his glory.

I want to encourage you today, dear friend, that there is nothing too complicated for God. God is powerful, has done mighty things, and will do mighty things for you and through you. Even now, in your darkness, I am standing with you. And I believe God is working on your behalf. He is for you.

As you meditate on the stepping stone of his miracles and his power over the impossible, I invite you to consider this:

T: Give the Lord thanks for what he has done and who he is in your life. Thank him for showing you that he is mighty and strong and is still a God who works miracles.

H: Pray that your faith and hope in Jesus will increase. Ask him to help you never to doubt his love for you. Trust that he is working things out for your good and his glory.

I: Ask God to help you to know that you are seen and heard and that he will respond to you. Pray that the Lord will answer your cries today and do what only he can do. As you pray, declare that you will see a miracle in this situation in the name of Jesus.

S: Even as you surrender to his will today, ask the Lord to help your unbelief. Ask him to help you trust His heart and plans for you, even when you can't see the way forward in this season of despair. Pray that he will increase your faith, give you peace, and help you overflow with joy while you wait on him today.

For this, I prayed.

GOD HAS RESPONDED

Then Jesus said to the disciples, 'Have faith in God. I tell you the truth, you can say to this mountain, 'May you be lifted up and thrown into the sea,' and it will happen. But you must really believe it will happen and have no doubt in your heart. I tell you, you can pray for anything, and if you believe that you've received it, it will be yours.'

MARK 11:22-24, NLT

As a mother raising miracle daughters here on earth, while waiting for the day I can embrace my miracle sons in heaven, I have wrestled with this verse.

When my sons were dying, I kept the faith. I prayed and believed, but still, they passed away. When doctors told us we would lose our daughters, I kept the faith, prayed, and believed, and they miraculously survived. After the different outcomes, I often asked myself if I did not have enough faith when praying for my sons. Nevertheless, with my daughters, there was something in me that could not stop praying. I just had to keep believing.

I realized that in living a life of unknowns, I had to keep choosing hope in a future I could not see. So, for me, there was no other alternative than to believe in God and trust that he would perform a miracle in my life to bring him glory, even if it did not look how I intended. And sometimes, this looks like asking others to come alongside you to pray for you and believe for you until you can pray and believe for yourself.

The irony is that I would never have had the joy of being a mother to my daughters if I didn't also have the pain of losing my sons. And while I sometimes buckle under the waves of grief for my boys, I cannot imagine a life without my girls.

My daughter Eliana's name means "God has responded." And indeed, God did respond to our prayers with the birth of our daughters.

If you need a miracle, I encourage you to keep believing and praying. And if you cannot pray today, I encourage you to invite a friend to pray and believe on your behalf.

God still does miracles. Sit at his feet and ask him to increase your faith and help your unbelief. He wants to hear from you and pour his love and peace over you. God wants to respond to you.

As you meditate on his response to our prayers of faith, I invite you to consider this:

T: Thank God for the miracle of his son Jesus and the power that still exists today because of him. Give him thanks for the promise that he always responds to our prayers.

H: Ask God to help your unbelief and increase your faith. Ask him to help you put all your hope in him.

I: As you sit at the feet of Jesus, tell him the desires of your heart. Cry out to him because he longs to hear from you.

S: Rest in the promise that God is faithful, and you can trust him. Ask him to help you keep believing as you surrender to him today.

For this, I prayed.

INFINITELY MORE

Never doubt God's mighty power to work in you and accomplish all this. He will achieve infinitely more than your greatest request, your most unbelievable dream, and exceed your wildest imagination! He will outdo them all for his miraculous power constantly energizes you.

EPHESIANS 3:20, TPT

When I was walking through a season of infertility, every time I went to the supermarket, I would park in the parking spot for expectant mothers.

I have spent my life believing that just as the flourishing trees have buried seeds, or my beloved peonies laid dormant for years before their flower, there is so much that we see today that had their foundation in the unseen. For me, there were many years of tears, trials, prayers, praises, and surrender among the many declarations that went forth in the desert. That parking spot was one of my desert declarations.

For many, seeing is believing, but "blessed are those who have not seen, yet have believed." (John 20:29, ESV)

Many had good intentions and did not want me to be disappointed, so they encouraged me to set low expectations and prepare for the worst, but I had crazy hope. I believed and trusted that God would bless me more than I could imagine. As I faced despair with all I could see, I focused on the dreams and unseen hopes. By parking in that spot, I chose to call those things that did not exist as if they did. (see Romans 4:17)

Dear friend, in this journey, because of the cross, we are fighting from a position of victory and breakthrough. We can trust in the God who moves miraculously in our lives. We can allow his power to energize us as we hope in him constantly.

With God, you don't need to prepare for the worst. You can trust his ability to supersede your wildest imaginations and dreams.

As you meditate on the stepping stone of his miraculous power, I invite you to consider this:

T: Thank God you do not need to plan for the worst with him. Praise him for the truth that you can always expect the best from him.

H: How does the truth of God's mighty and miraculous power lead you to have crazy hope and dream big dreams? Spend some time with God, sharing your wild ideas with him. He wants to hear them all.

I: If you are facing the impossible, make some desert declarations and praise God in your storm today.

S: How does God's infinite ability to accomplish your requests help you lay down your plans at his feet?

For this, I prayed.

NOW FAITH

Now faith is the assurance of things hoped for,
the conviction of things not seen.

HEBREWS 11:1, ESV

As we trusted God to get pregnant, we stood on faith that one day, we would finally receive a positive test result. There was no indication that it would ever happen, yet we believed. Every day, we had to keep declaring "Now faith" as we held on to this verse with assurance and conviction. But after losing our sons, it got harder to hang on to what we could not see. We wondered if it was meant to be.

Once we got pregnant with our daughters, we were thrilled until the dreaded day came when they asked us to choose. The doctors did not think it was medically possible for me to carry both girls, so they asked me to sacrifice Nia to save Eliana. But how could I make that choice?

I was already a mother to them both. How would I live with myself if I sacrificed Nia, and how would I live with myself if I lost them both, knowing I could have saved Eliana? It was an impossible choice that felt cruel because, after years of praying for the unseen, I once again had to put what I could now actually see (my daughters) in the hands of the God I trusted but could not see. Once again, I had to declare, "Now faith," in confidence that I could place my hope in the unseen.

In the following months, God carried my daughters, and he held and protected them even when it seemed like we made a foolish decision. Their lives are a wonder; every day, they prove that God still does miracles.

He did not have to do it to be good, but I am so grateful he did.

It is my deepest desire and prayer that the story of my daughters creates room in your heart to believe, trust, and pray again. I pray you can declare your faith once more with assurance.

God is a God of miracles. He is the same God, and he hasn't changed. He did it for me and can do it for you!

As you meditate on the stepping stone of his miracles, I would like to invite you to consider this:

T: Give the Lord thanks for being faithful and good. Even if he did nothing more, the gift of Jesus in our lives proves that God will always be good.

H: Pray that you never stop hoping, believing, and trusting in Jesus.

I: Even amid negative reports or facing the impossible, pray that God would increase your faith. Ask him to remind you that he is the same God who performed miracles years ago and has not changed. Pray that the Lord will give you wisdom in your current season, showing you the paths you should take through his word as you continue to trust that he will work it out for your good.

S: As you surrender today, pray that he will help you rest in his promises that are "yes and amen" (2 Corinthians 1:20). Give your worries to the Lord and ask him to fill you with his peace.

For your miracle, I have prayed.

TEN:

STONE
OF
freedom

STONE OF FREEDOM

Through all the years of chronic illness, infertility, miscarriage, and what I deemed my body's failure to hold on to our sons, I spent a long time telling myself that I was too broken, damaged, fat, sick, and scarred to be good. I felt inadequate and ashamed of this body I thought had repeatedly failed me.

Though my husband spent years reassuring me that I was beautiful, I rejected every positive thing he said. I couldn't fathom that he was telling me the truth. How could he be attracted to someone who was the opposite of everything society tells you to aspire to be?

As I battled with these thoughts about my body, I often could not find the words to pray. Instead, I would spend hours at a time in worship. And as I sang words of adoration to the Father amidst the cries of pain, I would lift my aching arms in surrender while bedridden. As I reflected on Romans 12:1, I realized that while presenting my bruised body as a living sacrifice, God accepted my worship.

This same body that cried out in worship was still standing and used by God to carry me when I thought I was falling apart. It was then that I started to embrace his freedom, as I finally started believing that my circumstances did not define my identity. The God who made me has never made a mistake, and he has looked at me with all my scars and declared that he has made me very good. (Genesis 1:31)

I still fight every day to keep walking in freedom. Getting pulled back into bondage is easy, especially with the comparison wars of social media. But I'm grateful that God never gave up on me despite my brokenness. Dear friend, it's okay if you are still struggling with accepting his freedom today because I know he won't give up on you.

I pray that you will start to view your scars through the eyes of the one who sees them as lines in a beautiful story of freedom. And that those same scars transform from a history of pain and shame into memorial stones of the overcoming power of Jesus. I pray they remind you to embrace his freedom.

As you meditate on the stepping stone of God's freedom, I invite you to consider this:

T: Lord, we thank you for being good; everything you create is good. Thank you for the freedom and victory found in you.

H: As you reflect on God's gift of freedom, how does this help you embrace hope and keep worshipping despite the brokenness in your body or other areas of your life?

I: Ask God to help you see the goodness in everything he has made, including yourself. Pray that he will help you embrace the identity that he has given you and that you will not fall into comparison.

S: As you surrender to God today, look at the beauty around you and spend some time in awe and wonder of his beautiful creations. Let his goodness lead you into freedom today.

For this, I prayed.

if the son
sets you free
you will be
free indeed

John 8:36

WHAT IS YOUR NAME

Rachel was about to die, but with her last breath she named the baby Ben-oni (which means 'son of my sorrow'). The baby's father, however, called him Benjamin (which means 'son of my right hand').

GENESIS 35:18, NLT

Names are important.

What names are you calling yourself?

Based on your circumstances, does your identity change?

What names has your heavenly Father given you?

When my daughter Eliana was very young, we noticed she had the gift of encouragement. I will never forget an interaction we had once in the check-out line of a hardware store. The cashier looked at her and remarked on how beautiful she looked in her dress. The cashier went on to say she wished she could look beautiful but couldn't wear dresses at her job.

"But your clothes don't make you beautiful," Eliana responded. "You are beautiful. And even if things change, that doesn't matter because beautiful is who you are, and you can't change who you are."

Friend, who are you? Whom does God say you are?

When tempted to call yourself other names based on your current season, your Father says this through scripture:

- You are a masterpiece. (Ephesians 2:10)

- You are made in God's image. (Genesis 1:27)

- You are altogether beautiful. There is no flaw in you. (Song of Songs 4:7)

When we embrace the identities our creator has assigned us, we can lay aside the bondage of shame and the disparaging names we speak over ourselves and walk in God's gift of freedom.

You are beautiful. Your Father delights in you. You don't need to change who you are.

As you meditate on the stepping stone of God's freedom you find in being who he has called you to be, I invite you to consider this:

T: Give God thanks that from the beginning of time, he created you in his image and called you good.

H: As you reflect on the names God has called you, think about the awe and beauty you see in him. How does it give you hope to know that the same beauty is also in you?

I: Ask your heavenly Father to help you always remember your identity is not dependent on your circumstances. Ask him to help you walk in freedom as you drop the weight of shame and pick up the love found in him as he calls you beautiful.

S: As you surrender to God today, write down one verse that reminds you of your beauty. Place it somewhere easily visible and declare his word over you as you walk in the freedom of embracing the names your Father has given you.

For this, I prayed.

REMARKABLY MADE

I will praise you because I have been remarkably and wondrously made. Your works are wondrous, and I know this very well.

PSALM 139:14, CSB

One of the features I disliked most about myself growing up was my smile. I have always had a gap in my teeth, and as a young child, I often heard I would need braces to fix it. Naturally, I saw my smile as flawed.

Well, I got braces and even had a retainer for a while. My smile was "fixed" until adulthood when the gap returned. I started hiding my smile in pictures and even asked my dentist for a referral to an orthodontist so I could try to fix this perceived imperfection once again.

As I embraced my entire body as remarkably made, I began to walk in freedom. I could no longer hide my smile. I realized I was always laughing and would get comments from others about them loving my smile.

As I embraced the freedom found in loving God's creation, it was as if he used the gap in my smile to fill the holes in my heart, and I couldn't contain the overflow. God was using the part of me I once hated as an instrument to show others they were accepted, beautiful, seen, and loved.

You, my friend, are remarkably and wonderfully made, and you have no flaws. Your every detail was intricately knitted by a loving

Father who longs for you to walk in freedom as you accept his beautiful creation—your very body—and use it for his glory.

I pray you will run in this freedom today, and when you glimpse yourself in the mirror, you will be smiling!

As you meditate on the stepping stone of his freedom found in the wondrous details of your body, I invite you to consider this:

T: Thank God for considering every detail of creation and making you remarkable.

H: If you are struggling with accepting freedom in the brokenness of your body today, ask God to fill you with his hope and joy. He sees you and longs for you to run into his embrace.

I: Pray that the Lord will enter the gaps in your heart. Ask him to help you smile again, even as you may face challenges in your body.

S: As you surrender to God today, ask him to remind you of his truth. Pray that as you rest in the delight he has over you, he will open your eyes and heart to receive his acceptance and love.

For this, I prayed.

IT'S NOT A DREAM

The angel struck him on the side to awaken him and said, "Quick! Get up!" And the chains fell off his wrists. Then the angel told him, "Get dressed and put on your sandals." And he did. "Now put on your coat and follow me," the angel ordered. So, Peter left the cell, following the angel. But all the time he thought it was a vision. He didn't realize it was actually happening.

ACTS 12:7–9, NLT

In the book of Acts Chapter 12, King Herod had already executed James and imprisoned Peter. The night before Peter's trial, he was sleeping in chains with a soldier on either side when an angel of the Lord appeared and freed him. However, even as Peter was walking in his freedom, he didn't believe it was real.

I think back to a difficult situation at my job. I was so miserable and stressed that it started affecting my health. I tried to find a way out, but every choice would leave our family in a financial bind. I felt trapped.

After much prayer, I was about to walk away when the Lord opened a miraculous door I had never seen coming. I got a better job that promised to relieve some of the stress and health challenges I had been experiencing. However, even as I stood in awe of what God had done, I didn't initially tell many people because I could not believe it was happening.

I was so hung up on the dream of freedom that I was not living in the reality of freedom.

Sometimes, we know we should be running free, but we gingerly hold this freedom as if it is a vision instead of living in the reality that the chains are gone.

"If the Son sets you free, you are truly free."

JOHN 8:36, NLT

Dear friend, I encourage you today to walk, run, and live in the reality that Jesus has set you free and then share that freedom with others.

As you meditate on the stepping stone of his freedom that is a reality, I invite you to consider this:

T: Lord, thank you for the gift of your freedom. Thank you for always showing up and providing a way of escape, even in the most challenging situations.

H: How does the reality of God's freedom give you hope you can share with others?

I: If you are in a season of bondage, imagine what freedom would look like for you today, then make your requests known to God. Pray that these visions will become a reality.

S: Like Peter rested in chains the night before his trial, pray God allows you to relax in him and that he be glorified even in this.

For this, I prayed.

NO BONDAGE, NO SHAME

It is for freedom that Christ has set us free.
Stand firm, then, and do not let yourselves be
burdened again by a yoke of slavery.

GALATIANS 5:1, NIV

My daughter Eliana says, "I'm sorry," all the time. She tries so hard to do everything perfectly, so whenever she does something wrong and we draw her attention to it, she will not stop apologizing and doesn't easily forget. There are times when, though forgiven, and we have all moved on from the incident, she will mention it months later and apologize again.

As I think about how hard it is for her to accept forgiveness fully, I think about how often I struggle to let go of my past sins and truly walk in freedom.

Jesus Christ has set us free. With his very life, he has paid the price for our sins, and we no longer walk in condemnation or the bondage that comes with keeping our focus on our faults.

The enemy wants to burden us by reminding us of our shortcomings, which is exhausting. But Jesus did not die on the cross for us to keep walking in shame, but so we could accept his freedom based on an intimate relationship with him.

God does not base the freedom he gives on our ability to live sinless but on the fact that we are broken people who cannot redeem ourselves. We are imperfect people who need a perfect Savior. We need Jesus!

Let's be intentional about standing firm each day as we cultivate a personal relationship with the one whose death is the foundation of our freedom. And let's accept this gift by forgetting what is behind us and move forward in his grace, mercy, love, and freedom!

As you meditate on the stepping stone of his freedom from the bondage of sin, I invite you to consider this:

T: Lord, I thank you for the gift of your son Jesus, whose death on the cross was payment for my sin. Because of him, I can walk in your freedom!

H: How does this freedom help you stand firm in the hope of Jesus and nurture your relationship with him?

I: Ask God to help you let go of past sins and to forgive yourself as he has forgiven you.

S: As you embrace this freedom, be intentional about spending some time each day developing your relationship with Jesus. He longs to hear from you and to remind you that you are no longer a slave, but you are his beloved child.

For this, I prayed.

UNTIL ALL ARE FREE

We will not hide these truths from our children; we will
tell the next generation about the glorious deeds of
the Lord, about his power and his mighty wonders.

PSALM 78:4, NLT

My daughters make me want to walk in freedom and love every
part of me because they are so free.

Growing up, I did not like my hair. It was super curly, and, in my
mind, it was not pretty. I wanted my hair to be long and straight,
and I spent thousands of dollars over the years trying to get "good"
hair.

And now, I am a mother of girls with super curly hair who both
absolutely love their hair.

As I look at the joy on my girls' faces after they get their hair done,
I cannot help but tell them of the creator who knit every detail of
them together so perfectly, including their hair. I tell them that as
a child, I was not as free as they are now. And I encourage them to
share this freedom with their children.

Our acceptance of the good deeds of our Creator, my friend, is how
we not only break free but stay free and teach the generations not
yet born to walk in freedom.

Regarding my children, I don't allow any negative words to be
spoken about their appearances. And I realize that as I guard the
freedom of my future generations, I must also accept this freedom
for myself.

Let's tell the next generation the glorious freedom available to us, a gift from the Father. And let's show them how to embrace the mighty wonder of our bodies as we walk in that freedom.

As you meditate on the stepping stone of his generational freedom, I invite you to consider this:

T: Lord, thank you for the mighty gift of freedom available to me and all my future generations.

H: Help me always share Jesus's hope and freedom with my children and grandchildren.

I: I pray that they would always see themselves the way Jesus sees them, as one of his mighty wonders.

S: May they always look to you and the truths of your Word and not the stereotypes of this world. Empower them to keep walking in freedom as they surrender to you, and may their hearts forever radiate your beauty to future generations.

For this, I prayed.

ELEVEN:

STONE
OF
grace

STONE OF GRACE

When our kids were first diagnosed with autism, I was bedridden from daily complications due to endometriosis. We also struggled to find a new church home and had few friends. I wrestled with how to be a good wife and mother as my children had so many needs that would be hard for me to fulfill when I was always in pain.

As we walked through a challenging time physically, emotionally, and spiritually, we grieved the life we thought we would have had after so many years of battling infertility. We didn't expect it to be so hard. God opened my eyes and heart to his love and kindness during our struggles. The grace of God carried us.

This grace from God kept us going when we didn't feel like we could survive another day. Sometimes, Andrew and I got frustrated and angry with each other, but God's grace towards us was constant. And as we experienced his grace, it allowed us to have grace for each other.

Grace is a gift of undeserved favor and kindness. It is given freely and reflects the heart of the Giver, not of the recipient.

I have always been uncomfortable when others commend me for being present for my husband and children amid pain because I know my ability to keep showing up in challenging times has nothing to do with my character and everything to do with his grace.

The journey of parenting children with special needs has been a story of dependence. Our children depended on us when they could not verbally communicate their desires. And when questions and lack of understanding threatened to overwhelm us, we relied on God's grace rather than our desire for answers.

As I rested in him, I realized his grace is sufficient and constant. I could always rely on his power to sustain me when I couldn't see what was around the corner.

> "Three times I pleaded with the Lord about this, that it should leave me. But he said to me, 'My grace is sufficient for you, for my power is made perfect in weakness.'"

2 CORINTHIANS 12:8–9, ESV

We are all walking through something hard. If you are not there today, something will likely come up tomorrow. Dear friend, we need the grace of God on the hard days when we can't carry the load ourselves. And we need this same grace on the not-so-hard days to help us be gracious to others as they go through difficult seasons.

I pray that you open your heart to receive God's gift of grace and give it to others.

As you meditate on the stepping stone of his grace, I invite you to consider this:

T: Lord, I thank you for the gift of your grace that you so freely grant to us in times of need.

H: Pray that God would help you not rely on your own strength but receive his gift of grace. May this be the foundation of your hope in the days ahead.

I: As you approach the throne of grace, share the desires of your heart with your heavenly Father.

S: Pray that God will give you the power to rest in the truth of his grace and faithfulness as you lay these burdens at his feet today.

For this, I prayed.

my grace is
sufficient for you,
for my power is
made perfect
in weakness

2 Corinthians 12:9

EVEN IN BROKENNESS

Rejoice with those who rejoice,
weep with those who weep.
Live in harmony with one another.

ROMANS 12:15–16, ESV

Throughout my years of infertility, I hosted multiple baby showers. It's hard to explain the wave of emotions I sometimes experienced in a single day. I would get so excited to celebrate the upcoming birth of another precious child in our community while simultaneously grieving the reality of my current circumstances.

The week before our sons passed away, we celebrated the birth of a little boy in our community. Exactly one week after we lost our sons, my sister gave birth to our nephew. For the remainder of that year, three other precious boys were born in our circle of friends, one of whom shares a name with my son Caleb. It seemed like there were boys everywhere. And with each passing year, as I celebrate the birthdays of so many born in the same year as our sons, I find myself holding on to moments of extravagant joy alongside overwhelming sadness.

I must admit there are times when the weight of grief washes over me. It is only through leaning on the grace of God that I can share in the happiness of others even as I continue to carry the heavy burden of loss. As I rest in this grace, I feel empowered to step back when needed or to seek support from my family and friends as we share our joys and sorrows in a space filled with the love of Jesus.

Even if you are walking through a tough time today, someone close to you may be celebrating. How do we live in harmony with each other during these extreme circumstances? How can joy and suffering coexist authentically?

You make room for hard and hope to coexist when you allow the grace of God to fill your heart and mind, and you give people this same grace in your weeping and your rejoicing.

We won't always get it right. But I am grateful that even in our brokenness, God has gifted us an overflow of his grace.

As you meditate on the stepping stone of God's grace as we relate to others, I invite you to consider this:

T: Give God thanks for the grace he freely gives us, even when we cannot give this grace to others.

H: As you reflect on this grace, allow it to fill you with hope as you weep and rejoice.

I: If you are struggling with feeling joy for others today, give it to God and ask him to heal your heart. If you need a friend who will suffer alongside you today, pray that God will send someone to sit with you as you weep.

S: As you surrender today, pray that Jesus will remind you that he is your best friend. And as you rest in him, receive his grace to strengthen you tomorrow.

For this, I prayed.

AFTER A LITTLE WHILE

And after you have suffered a little while, the God of all grace, who has called you to his eternal glory in Christ, will himself restore, confirm, strengthen, and establish you.

1 PETER 5:10, ESV

In my home country of Jamaica, we have the phrase "soon come." While the term is supposed to mean, "I'll be right there," if a Jamaican tells you "soon come," don't hold your breath. It could mean hours or days before you see them.

While we can use this phrase often with Eliana, we struggle to say the same thing to Nia. She only understands scheduled things. If you need her to wait, she wants you to give her an exact time, and she sets a timer. It is in everyone's best interest not to make her wait after the time has expired.

In some ways, we all have trouble waiting beyond our expectation of "a little while." While suffering, I have often wondered, is this duration measured in days, weeks, or months? Is it possible that this suffering will go on for years? It's hard not to get frustrated after our definition of "a little while" has passed.

But even if suffering lasts an entire lifetime, there is an expiration date when compared to the promise of eternity. When we are tired of affliction, 1 Peter 5:10 reminds us we are restored, confirmed, strengthened, and established by the God of all grace. The same grace that enabled us to survive yesterday is fresh, new, available today, and will be there tomorrow.

Whether you can set a timer on a particular season or if you are hearing "soon come" without a set date, I can assure you that your suffering will not last forever. But the grace of God will last for eternity. And this promise of his future grace is what I hope you will hold on to today.

As you meditate on the stepping stone reflecting the fullness of God's grace, I invite you to consider this:

T: Reflect on how God has restored, confirmed, strengthened, or established you. Give him thanks for his grace throughout your life.

H: As you reflect on this grace, allow the truth that he is the God of all grace to give you hope that this grace will be waiting for you tomorrow.

I: In your darkness today, pray that God will remind you that this will not last forever. Pray that your heart will be open to receive his grace when you are weary and tired of waiting.

S: As you rest in him, take some slow, deep breaths. Exhale your worries and inhale the grace of God you need today. As you do, be assured that you can draw from the well of his grace again tomorrow.

For this, I prayed.

COME BOLDLY

So let us come boldly to the throne of our gracious God.There we will receive his mercy, and we will find grace to help us when we need it most.

HEBREWS 4:16, NLT

Some school days are tough for Nia. After years of therapy, it doesn't happen as often anymore, but when she gets triggered at school, it gets really bad, extremely fast.

When she started third grade at a new school, we fully expected her to have several tough days, but it was the opposite. She had so many good days that we let our guard down. Then, out of nowhere, she got triggered, and she ran. While she has run away from adults before, this time, it felt different because she had been doing so well. When I heard the news, my heart was so sad because I almost forgot that she struggles to overcome the challenges of autism every day. Then I remembered that even with this, she continues working hard and has many good days.

When she got home that day, I asked her how her day went.

"It was the best day ever," she said. "Because first, it was really bad. Then I apologized, and everyone still loves me."

As I hugged her with tears in my eyes, it made me realize that we all mess up and have bad days. And on those days, I pray that we remember that this is not the end. Your actions do not define you. You are still loved, and there is an overflow of grace.

God is not a distant God. Because of Jesus, we can boldly enter into the throne room of a gracious God and receive compassion, mercy, and grace. I pray that when things get tough, you will remember that God's arms are open and waiting for you to approach him. I pray you feel him giving you a warm hug as he tells you he loves you.

As you meditate on the stepping stone of God's grace that you can receive as you boldly approach his throne, I invite you to consider this:

T: Give God thanks for the grace he extends to you at all times, on your good and bad days. Give thanks for the gift of his Son, Jesus, which allows us to approach his throne to receive this grace boldly.

H: Reflecting on this grace and the truth that God is not a distant God, how does this give you hope to forgive yourself instead of sitting in shame after you have struggled with sin?

I: As you thank God for his mercy and grace today, ask him to reveal the areas where you need to seek his forgiveness. Run into the arms of your Father and receive his compassion and love today.

S: As you rest in him, imagine God's arms around you. And as you take some deep breaths, breathe in God's love, acceptance, and grace.

For this, I prayed.

GRACE UPON GRACE

For from his fullness, we have all received,
grace upon grace.

JOHN 1:16, ESV

When you look at my daughter, you will see grace on display.
Initially, I thought I needed the grace to handle the challenges of
being a special needs mother, but I quickly realized it's Nia who
needs grace with me.

I have never been very patient; sometimes, I get frustrated when
she is not listening or responding. We learned a few years into
our journey with autism that my daughter has a processing delay.
It takes her longer to receive and understand the information
whenever we speak.

The problem is, because we thought she wasn't listening, we
would speak again, and it would only restart her processing time.
I can only imagine how frustrating it was for Nia to have people
constantly speaking at her without genuinely giving her a chance
to respond. But still, she gave us all grace. And while we know her
challenge, it is our human nature to forget when those around us
are different, and we tend to revert to what works best for us. But
every day, she shows us grace upon grace.

Each day, my daughter enters a world where many people see
her as different. She works extra hard to show up and show grace
to people who are not always kind to her. Some days are more
manageable, and on other days, you may catch her screaming or

retreating to a quiet place all alone because it cannot be easy to keep showering the world with grace.

Ultimately, we are all human, and repeatedly giving grace is hard. I thank the Savior who multiplies grace even when our sins multiply.

> Now the law came in to increase the trespass, but where sin increased, grace abounded all the more.

ROMANS 5:20, ESV

Jesus is full of grace, my friend. And he is waiting to shower you with grace today and more tomorrow. There is nothing you can do to earn this grace, and nothing on earth can separate you from it. I pray you will run into the rain of this grace today.

As you meditate on the stepping stone of the overflow of God's grace, I invite you to consider this:

T: Give thanks for the grace upon grace available to you. Praise God that our sins do not disqualify us from this grace, but we can return to him with a repentant heart to receive the grace that abounds.

H: As you reflect on this grace, how does this increase your hope in your compassionate savior, Jesus?

I: As you prepare to receive the grace of God today, ask him to show you any areas of your heart or your relationship with him that need repair. Ask him to help you hunger and thirst only for him and not the things of this world.

S: As you surrender to God today, ask him to help you always trust him. Ask him to deliver you from the cycle of sin and increase your dependence on him.

For this, I prayed.

GIVE GRACE

But grace was given to each one of us
according to the measure of Christ's gift.

EPHESIANS 4:7, ESV

In our family, we are always late. No matter how hard we try, we somehow still manage to be late more times than not. And we never want to be the ones to make excuses, so we apologize and sometimes endure the comments from others that, many times, leave us feeling ashamed.

The truth is, sometimes we are late because our daughter screamed all night. Other times, we are late because she wants extra bacon and can't focus if she doesn't finish breakfast. And then there are days when we sit and listen to them talk about their dreams. We remember the days they couldn't speak and now lose track of time listening now that they can talk. Sometimes, being late looks like one kid sneaking in an extra hug from her sister. They won't see each other all day at school, and she wants to reassure her that she will have a good day.

You don't know if someone is running late because things are falling apart or because they are living in an answered prayer. I have learned not to judge and to, instead, give grace.

Sometimes, grace looks like a warm smile; at other times, it looks like helping someone struggling.

I remember the first time we went on a plane with our daughters and a passenger looked at us as one of them started fidgeting. As I explained that she has autism and it's hard for her to sit still, he smiled and said, "It's okay with me." Sometimes, grace may look like showing compassion to others.

The grace of God is available in every detail, big or small, and in the same way, we get to be and give grace in a world that is hurting.

"Be kind to one another, tenderhearted, forgiving one another, as God in Christ forgave you."

EPHESIANS 4:32, ESV

Let's be kind and give grace, friends.

As you meditate on the stepping stone of God's grace and how this enables us to give grace to others, I invite you to consider this:

T: Thank God for his grace as he has forgiven us of all sins. Reflect on when you have received grace from a friend or a stranger.

H: As you reflect on the grace you have received, how does this increase your hope and faith that God will enable you to share this grace with others?

I: Ask God to show you someone in need of grace today. Pray that he will keep your heart soft and remind you of your need for grace as you interact with others.

S: Pray that God will keep you humble each day as you seek to honor the grace he has given you by extending grace to others.

For this, I prayed.

TWELVE:

STONE
OF
Joy

STONE OF JOY

After losing our sons, we sought joy despite our feelings. I could not survive the level of grief we were walking through without holding on to some form of joy, so I had to find it.

As I started looking for the light, I realized that on my darkest days, God's goodness, his light, and his mercy tracked me down, and his joy found me.

Christians tend to look for extravagant displays of God's goodness. We expect his joy to look a certain way. But often, joy does not come in the packages we imagine it will. The short lives of my sons taught me that you don't need much time to make an impact. They taught me you can hold on to joy, even in grief. While thoughts of their lives usually bring on tears, my unending love for them and the hope that I will see them again one day will always make this mother's heart leap with joy.

Life can be challenging, my friend. We live in a broken world, and life may not get easier as it transitions from one season to the next. So, I have decided to keep choosing the hard joys. I want to keep finding ways to make the simple things more significant than the complexities in this gift of life.

Sometimes, this joy is in the flicker of the candlelight, or it may be in the beauty of the spring flowers. I have noticed that when I focus on celebrating the abundance of God where my feet are planted, he always responds with glimpses of his joy.

"You crown the year with a bountiful harvest; even the hard pathways overflow with abundance. The grasslands of the wilderness become a lush pasture, and the hillsides blossom with joy."

PSALM 65:11-12, NLT

Our hearts can find joy even in the hardest of times. We find it in the one who always rejoices over us with songs of joy. I pray that even as you seek the heart of the Father, regardless of your current circumstances, he will fill you to overflow with his joy!

As you meditate on the stepping stone of his joy, I invite you to join me in this prayer:

T: Lord Jesus, I thank you for your joy that is complete. Thank you for pursuing us with your goodness, mercy, and joy, even in the darkest days.

H: Help us keep our eyes fixed on you, the source of all our hope. Help us cling to the promise of an eternity with you filled with unending joy.

I: In our current difficulties, help us put our trust in you, Jesus. Open our eyes to see glimpses of you and your joy in our daily lives. Show us our abundance in you right now, even if it does not look the way we planned.

S: As we give our worries to you today, we inhale "Even in the hard," and exhale "There is abundance," then inhale "Even in the wilderness," and exhale "We will blossom with joy."

For this, I prayed.

FULL OF JOY

Always be full of joy in the Lord. I say it again – rejoice!

PHILIPPIANS 4:4, NLT

Eliana has a huge personality. She is loud, curious, intense, and has the biggest heart. When Eliana meets you, she almost always asks your name, what makes you happy, and if you want a hug. We have sometimes tried to hold her back because she will even do this with strangers. She has told us that her mission in life is to love people and to "be joy."

Once, as we were leaving a waffle shop, Eliana stopped the server. We knew what was coming and tried to stop her—but before we could, she hugged the server, and we were apologizing. We explained that we were trying to get her not to be so bold, but in response, the server looked at Eliana with tears in her eyes and said,

"Stay bright. Stay bold. Stay extra. Don't shrink back. Keep filling the room. Never change who you are. I needed a hug from you today. I needed all of you to show up."

While we try hard to protect her from strangers and rejection, we realize that sometimes we don't see what she sees. People need people. People need us to be joy to one another.

It is hard to be joyful all the time. But it is possible to choose to be intentional about having an attitude of joy in the Lord.

> "Be cheerful with joyous celebrations in every season
> of life. Let your joy overflow!"

PHILLIPIANS 4:4, TPT

If the source of our joy is in the Lord, even in our weakness, we can look to him to access the joy.

I pray you walk in his joy today, and if you are struggling to find this joy, I pray someone shows up who can represent the joy of the Lord in your life today.

As you meditate on the stepping stone of his joy, I invite you to consider this:

T: Give God thanks for a joy that is not dependent on your circumstances. Ask him to remind you of when you truly felt his joy. As you hold on to that joy, pray that he will allow you to feel that again.

H: As you reflect on the joy of the Lord, ask him to remind you that he is your hope. As you think about the foundation of your hope being Jesus, how does this help you to find contentment in your circumstances as you view yourself in the light of eternity?

I: If you are currently in the midst of a storm, pray that the Lord would send someone your way who can share glimpses of his joy with you today.

S: As you surrender to Jesus, how can you "be joy" to someone else today? Even if you don't feel joyful in your circumstances, can you help uplift someone as you rejoice in the Lord?

For this, I prayed.

HIS JOY, YOUR STRENGTH

You make known to me the path of life;
in your presence there is fullness of joy;
at your right hand are pleasures forevermore.

PSALM 16:11, ESV

And do not be grieved,
for the joy of the Lord is your strength.

NEHEMIAH 8:10, ESV

Shortly after we lost our sons, we went back to church. I could not explain it, but I felt the need to be there. I must admit that while I was there, I was initially unable to pray or worship. I just showed up and sat there.

Week after week, as I continued attending, I realized I was finding joy in the presence of the Lord. Then, as his joy found me, I noticed it built up my strength.

If you are going through a tough time today, I encourage you to stay in community with people who can sit with you and lend you some of their strength and faith when you don't know where to turn. It could be in a church setting, with a smaller group of friends, or allowing someone to sit with you in your pain.

The enemy wants us to think we are all alone and no one cares about us. When we are in this state of fragility, it is hard for us to see the way out. We are not meant to go through this life alone. God dwells in the presence of his people, and our faith, hope, and joy grow in community with others. It is this joy that strengthens us for the journey ahead.

You are not alone, my friend, if you feel weak and without hope today. As in Hebrews 12:1, there is a cloud of witnesses waiting to embrace you as you seek the presence of the Lord. God loves you. He is for you. He is waiting for you, and in him where you will find joy.

As you meditate on the joy found in his presence, I invite you to consider this:

T: Lord, thank you for the fact that we are never alone. Thank you for the assurance that in you, we can have the fullness of joy and we will find strength.

H: As you prepare to receive this joy, ask God to open your eyes to show you the pathways of life. How does the assurance that this path leads to abundant joy fill you with hope?

I: Pray that God would lead you to a community that can stand with you. Ask God to give you a tangible sign of his presence to fill you with his joy in times of sorrow.

S: As you surrender to God today, I encourage you to allow yourself to receive as God shows up. That may look like going to church, or it may look like allowing the community of believers to shower his love on you right where you are at home. As the body of Christ shows up for you, pray that your heart will accept his joy and find strength.

For this, I prayed.

OVERFLOWING JOY

Now may God, the fountain of hope, fill you to
overflowing with uncontainable joy and perfect peace
as you trust in him. And may the power of the Holy
Spirit continually surround your life with his super-
abundance until you radiate with hope!

ROMANS 15:13, TPT

Some days, when I wake up feeling defeated, I call my dad. I have
the best dad.

One morning, I called him, and I cried like a baby. I could not stop
crying. After he listened, encouraged, and prayed with and for me,
the Holy Spirit started giving me hope.

While my dad did not have the answers to my problems, he
pointed me to the one who did. He reminded me that I have
survived hard things with God before and have seen him do the
impossible. He reminded me that as long as Jesus has risen, there is
hope, and if I trust in God, he will fill me with peace and joy.

I'm grateful I can still call my daddy and cry, even as an adult. It's
a reminder that I can still go to my heavenly Father and cry at any
age, too.

There are times when we find ourselves striving to get things done
on our own, and we find ourselves facing a tough challenge with no
way out. It leaves us hopeless, tired, and dejected. But God did not
create us to strive, but rather to depend on him and surrender our
hopes, dreams, and plans to him.

"Trust in the Lord with all your heart; do not depend
on your own understanding. Seek his will in all you do,
and he will show you which path to take."

PROVERBS 3:5–6, NLT

You can still run to your Father, my friend. He is waiting for you
to trust and rely on him. And when you do, he will fill you with an
uncontainable portion of his joy.

As you meditate on the joy found when our hearts trust in him, I
invite you to consider this:

T: Lord, thank you for the joy that overflows as we trust you.

H: As you reflect on this joy, thank God for being your fountain of
hope. As you imagine a fountain that continues to flow, how does
knowing that your source of hope will never run dry encourage you
today?

I: In your season of waiting, ask God to help you trust him more.
Ask him to remind you of the times he has not failed you, and pray
that he will help you to rely on him daily.

S: As you rest in God today, I want to remind you that he is not
like a man who can let you down. He is faithful, and his word is
true. You can run to him, and you can rely on him today. And as
you do, receive the gift of his indescribable joy.

For this, I prayed.

INEXPRESSIBLE JOY

You love him even though you have never seen him, though you do not see him now, you trust him; and you rejoice with a glorious inexpressible joy.

1 PETER 1:8, NLT

When I think of joy, I cannot stop imagining the face of my daughter, Eliana. She sees the world differently, in a way I have yet to see. While I tend to treat people through the lens of past hurts and experiences, she keeps showing up regardless of her interactions with people in the past.

In the third grade, Eliana had a rough start to her year. She met some unkind kids that left her feeling sad, but she continued to speak life into the people who hurt her. Eliana is the kind of child who walks bravely into rooms that typically drain your joy, and she embraces the person nobody sees until that person feels loved and seen.

I was not prepared for the difficulties she would face at school that year. But I was also not prepared for her heart to expand and for her arms to keep embracing others in the middle of it all. I pray every day that she never loses this joy.

Eliana's personality has allowed me to identify my skepticism and the walls I have put up around my heart. I look for people to demonstrate that they are trustworthy before I get too close. If someone seems too nice, I wonder if they are hiding something. Due to repeated hurts, I find it hard to trust people and reject kindness unless it is obvious.

But when I think of how God has been good to me, my love for him grows each day, and even though I can't see him, I believe in his love for me.

I pray you feel his love for you, too. I pray you receive this love without skepticism, and as you trust in him, I pray you can rejoice with a glorious, inexpressible joy that can come only from the Father.

As you meditate on the stepping stone of his glorious, inexpressible joy, I invite you to consider this:

T: Lord, thank you for allowing our hearts to overflow with joy as we have trusted you and your love for us.

H: Help us put our hope in you when times get hard, and never forget this joy you give that awaits us.

I: Lord, sometimes it is hard to believe you are for us when we suffer for a long time. Help us not to be skeptical and keep our eyes on you. We know that as we trust in you, we will not be put to shame (Psalm 25:3).

S: As you surrender to God today, think of how you have seen him work in your life. How does this help you continue trusting in him even though you cannot see him?

For this, I prayed.

COMPLETE JOY

I have told you these things so that my joy may be in you and your joy may be complete.

JOHN 15:11, CSB

As a family, we all have matching white shirts with the word "joyful" printed in vibrant colors. We wore them for a photo shoot once because it represented our desire as a family always to speak joyfully. Since then, I have kept the kids' shirts at the back of their dresser drawers. I was trying to hold on to them for as long as possible and didn't want them to get stained.

One day, Nia found the shirt and put it on. I did not realize until she asked for hot chocolate later that day. I cringed when I saw her in that white shirt because I knew what would happen. I made her promise to hold it with two hands. She promised not to make a mess, but I bet you can guess how that turned out.

She was enjoying her hot chocolate so much that she had to get every last drop, and from what I could see, the shirt enjoyed it, too. They were both a mess.

As I looked at her face, she was satisfied, happy, and filled with delight. I realized that while it was a total mess, she was joyful. And as I watched her smile I was also basking in immense joy.

That unexpected moment of complete joy was visible and bright enough to wipe out any stain.

The joy I experienced at my child's pleasure is the joy that awaits us when we abide in Jesus. As we stay close to him and remain in an intimate relationship, the joy that flows is spontaneous, overwhelming, and complete. And this joy is enough to penetrate any stains that may threaten to defeat us.

Our God is a God of joy! And this joy is not dependent on your circumstances. The joy of the Lord is there when things are going well, and it is there in the midst of the mess of life when sometimes all you can see are what looks like chocolate stains on a white shirt.

I pray that your joy will always be complete in him!

As you meditate on the stepping stone of his complete joy, I invite you to consider this:

T: Lord, thank you for continually filling us with your joy. Thank you for your joy, which is available to us even in our mess.

H: As you reflect on the complete joy of the Lord, pray this joy will always give you hope.

I: If you feel crushed on every side, pray you will stay close to the Lord. Pray you will abide in him and not go astray.

S: As you rest and abide in God today, pray you will be intentional about continuing to build an intimate relationship with him. Pray you will always overflow with his complete joy.

For this, I prayed.

i have told you
these things so that
my joy may be in you
and your joy
may be complete

John 15:11

ACKNOWLEDGEMENTS

To my constant, my husband Andrew, thank you for not giving up on me. When we first met each other at sixteen years old, it took me a few minutes to figure it out but you knew immediately that we would spend our lives together. Then years later when you proposed in the middle of an intense argument, you promised that you would never leave when things got hard, and you've been here every step of the way. Thank you for being my best friend.

To my miracles that are resting in the arms of Jesus, thank you for making me a mother. Noah, Caleb, and Micah, I am so proud of you. Your short time on this earth changed the way I live my entire life. You have made me a better wife, mother, and friend. You have made eternity so real to me, and I cannot wait to hug you again. One day closer my sweet boys.

To my precious blessings Eliana and Nia, you are our greatest gifts. There were days when the only thing that broke the silence in our home was the sound of my tears. I longed for the day when the giggles and squeals of little children would fill these rooms and our hearts. Thank you for completing our family. You show me every day what it means to persevere and overcome adversity. You are funny and kind, and you both give the best hugs. Being your mama has been my highest calling and greatest joy.

To my parents, siblings, and the rest of my family, thank you for always believing in me. Daddy and Mommy, thank you for always pointing me to Jesus. Your faith has been a continuous source of inspiration. Kirk, you passionately enjoy each day of your life, and the way you never give up on your dreams is to be admired. Delina, thank you for speaking life into my hardest days. In some ways, you are my little big sister and I am so proud of the mother, wife, and sister that you are. You are one of the strongest women I know.

To my dearest friends, thank you for literally sitting with me on the floor. You have painted rooms, brought meals, been intentional with weekly video calls, and cried with me when you had no words. Thank you for entering into my pain and being the hands and feet of Jesus. You have continued to remind me that I am not alone. Thank you for praying me through the darkness and for cheering me on. Your support, faith, and love have truly pulled me across the finish line of this book and continue to keep me going on this journey of life.

To my friends at Go and Tell Gals, my first editor Kaitlin, and book coach Morgan, thank you for being so kind. You encouraged me to keep going in my calling when I wasn't sure this was even a book at all. Thank you for always saying you were proud of me. I needed to hear that more than you would ever know. To Called Creatives Publishing who accepted this manuscript and decided to take a chance on me, thank you for all your hard work, design, and excitement in helping to make this book a reality.

And to my chief Cornerstone and Savior, thank you for showering me with your goodness. Thank you for being my rock and for your presence that has been with me always. Thank you for pouring these words into my heart, and for how you will use them for the good of the one that so desperately needs them, and for your glory. Indeed, none of my suffering has been wasted.

Made in the USA
Middletown, DE
17 November 2024